GROW

MW00627973

"Andy's ability to focus on what not to do is a unique approach to thinking about starting or running your business. I have had the opportunity to see Andy in action. He brings passion and experience and has been able to put that into his very engaging book. Do yourself a favor and read the book. You don't want to be an example of what not to do."

—*Michael Coles*
Co-Founder, Great American Cookies
Former CEO, Caribou Coffee

"Boost your entrepreneurial IQ while learning how to avoid costly mistakes with this informative book. Andy expertly lays out a highly engaging, practical road map for business growth and success that can quickly be put into action by most every business leader. Andy's techniques and tools worked well at the high growth Inc. 500 firm where we were both employed, and they will work for you too."

—*Brian Bellew*
Former Managing Director and Principal
Avison Young

"Andy has incredible insight and a special love and passion for entrepreneurship and business growth. I have enjoyed brainstorming as I build Venture Atlanta. In this book, with practical tools, methodologies, and case studies, Andy truly gets to the heart of what it takes to grow your business and, more importantly, avoid costly mistakes. I guarantee anyone thinking about becoming or currently is an entrepreneur will learn something from this book. I look forward to continuing to learn from him."

—*Allyson Eman*
CEO, Venture Atlanta

"As a company executive and client of Andy's, I appreciate his systemic, pragmatic, and results-driven approach. In this book, Andy uses straightforward language and illustrations to demonstrate how to grow your business and avoid costly mistakes. These expert lessons and ideas can be applied to your company with dramatic results."

—Mike Kingzett
Sr. Director, Lean and Continuous
Improvement, Air Methods Corporation

"We often forget that solid fundamentals—singles and doubles—win World Series. Andy's book is a great touchstone for any executive seeking to grow their business's top and bottom line as it drives home the critical importance of successful execution of your business's fundamentals."

—Tim Riordan
Director, Enterprise Procurement and
Support Services, Ultimate Software

"If you would like to be more successful, win more business, make more money, and scale a business the correct way quickly, then read this book. Andy takes a deep dive leveraging his thirty-year real-world business experiences and delivers a clear message here in one package on growing a business the right way. Well worth the read."

—Ryan Bowie
Senior Vice President, ICON Commercial Interests

GROW LIKE A PRO

Michael & Rich:

I hope you enjoy the book and that it inspires you and others to Grow Like A Pro.

Best,

Andy

GROW LIKE A PRO

Lessons from a 2X Inc. 500 Executive

Andy Goldstrom

Alpharetta, GA

ISBN: 978-1-63183-858-3 - Paperback
eISBN: 978-1-63183-859-0 - ePub
eISBN: 978-1-63183-860-6 - mobi

Library of Congress Control Number: 2020908839

Printed in the United States of America   0 5 1 1 3 0

♾This paper meets the requirements of ANSI/NISO Z39.48-1992 (Permanence of Paper)

Cover design by Alaka Oladimeji Basit, Leedigital
Cover photo by Kenji Kubota Photography
Editing by Ann Deiterich/WriteWordForYou LLC

To my late father, Steve Goldstrom,

who always encouraged me to pursue my entrepreneurial dreams.

I can't change the direction of the wind,
but I can adjust my sails to always reach my destination.

—Jimmy Dean

A bend in the road is not the end of the road
. . . unless you fail to make the turn.

—Helen Keller

CONTENTS

DEVELOP THE RIGHT PARTNERSHIPS

MANAGE FINANCES

OPERATE EFFICIENTLY

TRACK PERFORMANCE

DEVELOP AN EXIT PLAN

FOREWORD

As director of Georgia State University's Entrepreneurship & Innovation Institute, and in my prior work as vice president of the Metro Atlanta Chamber, I have had the opportunity to meet and collaborate with numerous founders and executive leaders from all over the world. In both the public and private sectors, I have learned and witnessed what is required to develop and maintain relationships and deliver on the promise. Andy Goldstrom exemplifies this kind of person.

I first met Andy when I joined Georgia State University in the fall of 2018. At the time, in addition to his consulting practice at Midcourse Advisors, he was exploring the possibility of teaching an introductory entrepreneurship course to undergraduate students. He was one of the first people to reach out and offer a helping hand as I adjusted to my new role and environment. It was an early indicator of how lucky our students are to have him as an instructor.

Twice a year, we hold a business model competition for our two hundred or so students who are enrolled in the introductory entrepreneurship course that Andy ultimately signed on to teach. Each instructor has the opportunity to select a team he or she has mentored during the semester to compete for bragging rights, a little capital, and a spot on a launchpad that can help take their business idea to the next level. In the first semester Andy taught the course, his team took home the top prize. Andy has since taught the more advanced entrepreneurship class, Product-Service Design for New Ventures, and been just as effective.

We know these teams don't win the competition alone—they win it with the help of committed and experienced instructors who go above the call of duty to prepare them for the competition. Those seem to be hallmarks of Andy's approach to everything he does. He is deeply committed to building productive relationships with people—including his students, colleagues, business partners, and members of his team—and elevating those with whom he is associated and anything of which he is a part.

It's inspiring to work with such a successful executive and entrepreneur who is genuine, thoughtful, and patient, and often chooses to see and address challenges through a lens of humor. Our students are incredibly fortunate to learn from an experienced professional who has practiced the art of starting and scaling businesses, and now, so too will you. Like our students, you'll also be exposed to leadership techniques from someone who sets high expectations of those around him and then accompanies them every step of the way to help them achieve, and more often than not, exceed those expectations.

As higher-education institutions, nonprofit organizations, governments, and the private sector continue to invest in building programs and infrastructure to support entrepreneurs and stimulate innovation to drive economic growth, we must remember that many start-ups still fail. We also must note that although existing businesses may have more resources than start-ups, money and time are finite, so taking the right approach is paramount.

This book and its emphasis on sustained growth and scalability make it an invaluable and timely resource that will allow us to reap the intended outcomes of economic growth and positive societal impact. For the aspiring or seasoned entrepreneur or established business leader, making mistakes is part of the game, but this book will remove many of the obstacles in the path to sustainable growth of your business.

Sincerely,
Dr. Jennifer Sherer
Director, Entrepreneurship & Innovation Institute
Georgia State University

INTRODUCTION

"Growth is always essential. Running any
company, you want to make sure you're
growing, putting in place all of the right
structure to be able to ensure growth."

—Susan Wojcicki
CEO of YouTube

Starting a business is hard. It takes ingenuity, vision, and passion, and involves taking risk as well. If there's a problem that you, as an entrepreneur, can solve via a product or service where customer demand exists, odds are more in your favor that you can achieve a successful launch.

Growing a business is far more complex, and in some ways more challenging, than your launch. As soon as the company grows beyond a handful of people, protocols, systems, reporting, and communications must change. Failure in that regard thwarts growth and could potentially lead to outright failure. Additional challenges occur when founding owners can't let go and delegate to others.

Many business leaders believe that if they work hard and make more good decisions than bad, they will succeed. Many do, but most do not.

The reason? Some mistakes are so costly that they can derail your business or bankrupt it. Therefore, all business leaders should know that avoiding critical mistakes enhances their chances of success.

As a result, if you're an entrepreneur with a vision to grow your company—from start-up to stable small company, or from small to midsize and beyond, and to take your unique value proposition and substantially increase revenue and profitability—this is the book you should read.

Grow Like a Pro is designed to help you make the moves that keep you focused on your business goals and avoid the common blunders too many leaders make. I will show you how to avoid the mistakes that cost you time, money, and in some cases, your business. I will discuss the challenges leaders face, including how to:

1. Identify a problem
2. Target the right customer
3. Launch profitably
4. Manage the sales process
5. Lead the right team
6. Develop the right partnerships
7. Manage finances
8. Operate efficiently
9. Track performance
10. Develop an exit plan

To start and succeed over the long term, you have to focus on the problem you can solve for your customer and then clearly identify the solution, your unique offering and experience, and the buyer's true cost of inaction.

You need to have capable employees in the right positions, a development and training process, a reporting system, and a compensation system that enables you to keep staff. In building your team—the human capital—first and foremost, you have to have a plan that allows your staff to have an impact and see their own path for opportunity within your company. With that in place, you've increased the likelihood of your team sticking with you. If not, people (perhaps, millennials especially) aren't afraid to try something different and will head for the door.

Companies also position themselves for growth by hiring correctly in the first place. Hire for attitude rather than skill. You can always teach a skill, but you're unlikely to eliminate a poor attitude.

You should also look to employ people with different approaches and personalities. There are visionary types as well as the "get 'er done," checklist/organized, and relational types of employees. In order for teams to be effective, you need a variety of personality types that you—as the leader—manage.

Once you're beyond the start-up phase, the role of the entrepreneur and senior leadership changes as you become a servant to the team, making sure the team succeeds. When the team succeeds and grows, the company succeeds and grows. Beyond the start-up phase, it's time to let go of the reins for the sake of growing the company.

When your employees are happy and not being micromanaged, you're more likely to have a sales approach that scales and one with which stakeholders are comfortable and, as a result, far more likely to say yes and get to yes faster.

Today, companies are incredibly sophisticated in how they purchase. There are more systems, stakeholders, and governance involved in buying decisions. The days of unilateral decisions made with deals struck on the golf course are nearly over. Too many sales reps focus on extolling themselves and their companies. However, a single buying stakeholder can give a thumbs-down and derail the deal. In today's business environment, it's unusual for one person to be the sole decision maker, so you must focus on the right prospective customer.

Financially, it is important to vigorously manage cash flow on a daily basis. The primary reason companies go out of business is because they run out of cash. Many optimistic leaders deliver a good new product or service but fail to monetize it in a timely manner, unable to align revenues with associated expenses.

Therefore, it is important to invest in opportunities that have a high chance of success where you can objectively assess the risks and know how to leverage other sources of cash to propel your business.

Operationally, as Michael Gerber, author of *The E Myth*, has aptly suggested, people need to run the systems and the systems need to run the business. In addition, the Pareto principle is timeless. Focus on what's important—what's urgent and impactful. In operations, as in sales, focus on the 20 percent that will yield 80 percent of the results you want.

Finally, I've seen companies soar simply by implementing the right systems in the right place to support the growth. They secured the right clients and staff, had a consistent approach to sales along with dependable cash flow, and had operational processes that could scale—everyone using the same tools and technology to execute the same way. With this in place, business owners can focus on vision, strategy, and partnerships and spend less time on day-to-day operations. Owners who continue to focus on every aspect of their businesses often end up closing their companies.

Throughout this book, I'll cover ways that will enable you to create and put into place the processes that will enable consistent, repetitive, and scalable growth and allow for greater innovation for even more success. Often, due to inexperience of the owner or staff, when a company begins to grow, one or more processes break because they were not properly designed, not working, or not scaling in tandem. When a process breaks, you become reactionary. Once growth begins, most entrepreneurs fail to focus on growing *correctly* and managing performance. In fact, they often don't recognize this failure or refuse to accept it. They're fighting fires every day and don't realize that making an investment in creating consistent processes that will allow for better execution and improved customer satisfaction will let them to extinguish their fires forever.

Unfortunately, many executives wait too long to reach out for help. Some think they're doing well enough only to have that growth topple the business. Perhaps they lost a huge client they'll never regain. Or maybe some key team members decided to pursue other opportunities. These employees are tough to replace and it's equally tough to get their replacements up to speed. Or one day, you have plenty of cash and the next you are struggling to make ends meet. If you have the right approach, you can avoid these pitfalls.

I've been an executive leader at two Inc. 500 companies and I've seen these types of challenges firsthand. I've also taught entrepreneurship at the university level. In working with dozens of companies that have struggled with achieving their goals, I've seen what it takes to properly start and also grow a company. That's why I've written this book. I want to show you the right way to grow your company so it's far more profitable than you ever imagined.

My career has spanned nearly thirty years in organizations both big and small. I've also been a part of corporate teams, some of which have had global footprints. Some of the companies I've worked at include USI, a corporate real estate outsourcing firm at which I was the managing director and Southeast regional president that became an Inc. 500 company and was then acquired by Johnson Controls, where I served in the same capacity; International Environmental Management (IEM), a recycling firm focused on retail real estate owners where I served as its president that also became an Inc. 500 company (as part of Oakleaf Global Holdings) and was then acquired by Waste Management; and Deutsche Bank, a global investment bank where I served as a global director.

As a result, I'm not simply espousing B-school jargon; I'm sharing my world experience of starting and growing companies several times over.

If you're in any kind of services business with the opportunity to grow (or one that is growing without the proper infrastructure), I've been there and know what leads to success. I know how to make it work. And if you manufacture or distribute a product, the same rules apply. I've made mistakes, so I know what it takes for you to avoid making those same errors.

I've also worked in strong economic cycles as well as very weak ones. As this book is being published, we are in the throes of the coronavirus pandemic. The tools and methodologies in this book become that much more applicable, and with even more urgency. In fact, I've included several assignments you can put to work now. Please take advantage of this opportunity to take the time and do the work.

No matter where you might find yourself today—whether you

are headed in the wrong direction or not heading anywhere at all—I want to help you change course and start accelerating the right way. Don't let your pride get in the way, thinking you can figure it all out and keep your hands in everything. And don't be afraid to change course, hanging on to a sinking ship until it hits bottom. It's time to cut your losses or rev up your efforts and start growing. By the time you finish this book, you will be able to implement key strategies to position your company for effective and successful growth.

Let's dive in!

IDENTIFY A PROBLEM

Chapter 1

WHAT PROBLEM ARE YOU SOLVING?

"Every breakthrough business idea begins with solving a common problem. The bigger the problem, the bigger the opportunity."

—*Michael Dell*
Dell Corporation Founder

In 1975, Sony introduced the Betamax video standard. It was a technological advance that enabled recording of live events, movies, and television shows. Sony management believed its technology was so advanced that it would dominate the market. Therefore, Sony would charge a premium for the products.

However, just a year later, JVC recognized Sony had failed to address a major problem—the Betamax format provided for only up to one hour of video recordings, which was one hour less than the duration of most movies. JVC created the VHS format, which solved this problem and was also less expensive and easier to implement. Sony's Betamax was soon history.

Customers want solutions, but there are steps you must put in place before you can develop the best solution or even the right solution. In the past, successful businesses experienced growth based on good business sense, as we did at USI. Those entrepreneurs who possessed the best business sense soared; those with lesser sense grew more slowly and from a lot of expensive (both time and money) trial and error . . . or they failed completely. Now, there is a more refined process that you can follow to help ensure greater start-up success.

Many businesses launch because individuals have an idea or a specific skill on which they want to capitalize. They have a dream about how they can change the world and create their own success; they invest plenty of money and elbow grease into bringing their vision to fruition. The dream of entrepreneurship certainly isn't new.

However, initially focusing on your solution is a backward approach and, even with a formal business plan, is unlikely to lead to a successful launch.

A great solution is completely and utterly irrelevant if it isn't addressing a corresponding problem. *The problem must come first.* No matter how talented you may be, and no matter the amount of passion you put into your business, if you are not solving a problem that customers truly have and care about addressing—as opposed to one that you imagine they have or that only a very small handful of people experience—your business will either never expand beyond the start-up phase or you will struggle to achieve the growth you envision. Developing a solution is far easier than identifying a suitable problem.

Enter the Business Model Canvas (BMC).

With the BMC approach, you first identify the problem, the customer, and the unique value proposition. This represents the what, who, and how. Once you have identified these three factors, you can then determine the solution. This is a far leaner approach to a business launch that eliminates wasted time, assets, inventory, etc.

The BMC Strategy is what I teach at Georgia State University, where I am a part-time instructor. I show my students how to focus on starting a business by testing the idea, including validating both the problem (does it really exist) and then the solution (is it what customers want and are willing to pay for).

At my consulting company, Midcourse Advisors, this is a key tool for any new service or product development initiatives.

The BMC isn't just for start-ups, however. As your business evolves, the model forces you to think about ongoing adjustments that you may need to make to the business.

At each phase of growth, you
should continually ask:

Does the problem I identified before still exist?

Are there different problems or nuances
that need to be addressed now?

Does my solution still uniquely solve the problem
or does it need to be updated and adjusted?

The Lean BMC (adapted by Ash Maurya from Alexander Osterwalder's original BMC) uses the same building blocks, but in a logical and process-driven way rather than linearly. Looking at the BMC in Figure 1-1, you might be tempted to begin in the upper left and work your way across, determining your solution early in the process. That's getting the cart before the horse.

The Lean BMC

PROBLEM	SOLUTION	UNIQUE VALUE PROPOSITION	UNFAIR ADVANTAGE	CUSTOMER SEGMENTS
Top 3 Problems	Top 3 Features	The single, clear, compelling message that states why you are different and worth buying!	Can't be easily copied or purchased	Target customers
	KEY METRICS Activities to measure		**CHANNELS** Path to customers	

COST STRUCTURE	REVENUE STREAMS
Customer Acquisition Costs Distribution Costs Hosting People Etc.	Revenue Model Lifetime Value Revenue Gross Margin

PRODUCT	**MARKET**

Figure 1-1

As I mentioned, the lean approach to employing this BMC is to forego attempting to follow this chart in a linear or left-to-right fashion. Yes, first you must determine the problem, but developing your solution is *not* the next step. Now consider this Lean BMC version, Figure 1-2.

The Lean BMC Sequencing

PROBLEM Top 3 Problems	SOLUTION Top 3 Features	UNIQUE VALUE PROPOSITION The single, clear, compelling message that states why you are different and worth buying!	UNFAIR ADVANTAGE Can't be easily copied or purchased	CUSTOMER SEGMENTS Target customers
1	4	3	5	2
	KEY METRICS Activities to measure		CHANNELS Path to customers	
	8		9	
7	COST STRUCTURE Customer Acquisition Costs Distribution Costs Hosting People Etc.		REVENUE STREAMS Revenue Model Lifetime Value Revenue Gross Margin	6
	PRODUCT		**MARKET**	

Figure 1-2

As you can see, Step 2 is to determine which customers have your defined problem, followed by your unique value proposition—the primary reason those customers will want to purchase from you. Only when those three elements are clearly defined should you begin working on the solution that will address the stated problem.

Keep in mind you may not hit on the best or even the right solution at the start. Continue to ask questions of the customers you defined in the second step and apply what you learn from them to develop the solution that becomes the "golden egg" for a successful launch and ongoing growth.

Only after you've taken the first four steps in the lean approach to a business launch will you consider how you might market to find more customers, develop your revenue streams, examine costs, and create metrics by which to measure—all factors that previously played a much bigger role at the start of the traditional business plan.

This methodology has been used for about a decade, and it's a good way to validate a new business as well as new products and services that you may develop before launching those.

REAL-WORLD EXAMPLES

At USI (before this method was defined and charted), we started by actually securing customers *before* we launched the business, so we mitigated our risk, validated our solution, and secured cash flow, actually following a very similar approach to the Lean BMC. We didn't simply plant a flag in the ground and announce our solution. Prior to launch, we proved that we had a market for the solution we were proposing. We observed that the savings and loan crisis in the late 1980s created an economic retraction which created the need for cost savings and staff flexibility. Expertise was still needed, however. So, we led a wave of outsourcing of real estate services based on this dynamic.

To help you better understand the BMC model, the following Figure 1-3 is the original BMC for Airbnb. Note there are two problems being addressed, providing an even more compelling value proposition.

AirBnB Business Model Canvas

PROBLEM	SOLUTION	UNIQUE VALUE PROPOSITION	UNFAIR ADVANTAGE	CUSTOMER SEGMENTS
Guests want to: • Feel a part of the local community • Get a unique insider's experience • Go to various destinations • Reduce expenses	Virtual platform with mobile app capabilities and network community of people involved	Hosts profit by renting out spaces, get insurance from Airbnb and get free photoshoots of their property.	• Host incentive • List once • Ease of use • Profiles • Design & brand	• Hosts • Guests • Photographers
Hosts want to: • Rent space for extra money • Share or provide unique experiences for guests	**KEY METRICS** • Active community growth rates • Annual booking targets • User reviews	Guests book with a local host to get an insider's experience and can choose from a variety of prices, destinations and housing options.	**CHANNELS** • Website • Mobile app • Social media • Word of mouth • Digital marketing • Affiliate model	

COST STRUCTURE	REVENUE STREAMS
• Technology • Employee salaries • Photographer fees	3% commission from hosts on every booking 6–12% commission from guests on every booking

PRODUCT	**MARKET**

Figure 1-3

As you can see, Airbnb identified a problem. Their founders determined travelers wanted more choices and a more intimate experience while hosts wanted to monetize excess spaces.

To further understand the BMC model, Figure 1-4 is the BMC for USI. Our customers wanted more strategic management capability, which would drive tangible savings. The unique value proposition was truly unique and actually disrupted and changed the industry.

USI Business Model Canvas

PROBLEM	SOLUTION	UNIQUE VALUE PROPOSITION	UNFAIR ADVANTAGE	CUSTOMER SEGMENTS
Companies need to save money through outsourcing and more strategic management of the corporate real estate function.	On-site, fully integrated real estate teams that reduce cycle times, save money, and best align real estate and operational needs.	Expertise, flexibility, and objectivity all delivered at a cost at or less than they could provide it themselves.	• Employees are paid a salary and benefits, so their behaviors are in line with the client's best interests. • Our process and technology applications are industry disrupters that enable great value.	Companies with large, disbursed portfolios of real estate they occupy.
	KEY METRICS • New installation launch timing & cost • Hard savings calculations • Incremental sales as a result of locational strategies • Reduced employee churn from occupancy strategies	Tenant-only representation ensures client/service provider alignment.	**CHANNELS** • In-house sales force • Complementary back-office companies • Industry trade groups	

COST STRUCTURE	REVENUE STREAMS
• Employee salaries and benefits • Technology • Marketing	• Fixed fees • Commissions

PRODUCT	MARKET

Figure 1-4

Using a BMC, rather than starting with a Plan A, you can actually start with a plan that works. Too many entrepreneurs start by asking if a product *can* be built. The real question to ask is whether it *should* be built and whether a sustainable business can be developed around the imagined products and services.

> ## Don't ask if a product can be built. It's more important to ask whether it should be built and whether a sustainable business can be built around this product and related services.

The lean approach to a business launch is not about spending less money or less time. As in lean manufacturing, it's about eliminating waste. It takes time and effort to create and validate a BMC. But it is time and effort well spent. Once you eliminate waste, in both time and investments, you'll find that you ultimately reach success and growth faster with a far healthier bottom line because you've taken the time from the outset to clearly identify the problem that customers truly face and for which they are willing to pay you for the solution. With that problem identified, you can employ your solution and continue the process for exponential growth.

ASSIGNMENT
> Time to pause and put what you learned to work.
>
> Draft a BMC for your business. You can download a template at www.midcourseadvisors.com/growlikeapro.

PARAMETERS FOR PROBLEM SOLVING

There are a few key parameters you should consider when identifying a relevant problem.

First, is the problem a pain point you have experienced? For example, Sara Blakely invented Spanx when she couldn't find pants that properly fit her. Gary Erickson got the idea for Clif Bars on a day-long, 175-mile bike ride, for which he packed a variety of energy bars and wasn't satisfied with the taste or nutritional contents. If you can identify a pain point either directly or indirectly, there is a good chance that others may also have the same pain that can then be validated.

Identifying a workplace pain point for which you can provide better products or services to your customers can also be quite effective because you have direct experience and can secure direct feedback.

In any event, you don't need to look too hard or far. There are problems and opportunities that can be identified in your everyday life.

Second, once you have identified a potential problem you wish to pursue further, make sure it is big, unique, and addressable and implementable at the right time. Stephen Schwarzman, chairman of Blackstone, the world's largest asset management company, says that if you and your company are going to invest the time and resources to grow and are willing to embrace the associated risk, you might as well do it big since it often takes as much effort to solve a small problem as it does a big one. That's also known as a BHAG, or Big Hairy Audacious Goal. Nelson Mandela, the former South African president, urged us to believe "There is no passion to be found playing small—in settling for a life that is less than the one you are capable of living."

Schwarzman also suggests you should be differentiated, as your chances for success are less if you don't stand out from the competition. Your solution also needs to be timely. Though big and unique, streaming video wasn't opportune until broadband was developed to provide the capacity to stream.

Finally, your offering should be unique and also valuable. According to Guy Kawasaki, a Silicon Valley–based venture capitalist, if someone doesn't want to purchase a product or service to solve a pain point, it isn't worth doing.

As Figure 1-5 illustrates, the Sweet Spot is the place you want and need to be. When both valuable and unique, you can more easily penetrate your market while commanding a premium price.

The Sweet Spot

Figure 1-5

PRO POINTERS

- Developing your solution in the form of a product or service before clearly defining the problem is putting the cart before the horse.

- The Business Model Canvas is a leaner approach to a successful business launch than the traditional business plan.

- You may not develop the best solution at the start. Continue to ask questions of your customer base to learn more about the problem.

- Continuing applying the BMC model for new products and services that you may develop before launching those.

- Don't ask if a product can be built. First ask if it *should* be built.

- If you can identify a pain point, either directly or indirectly, others have probably also experienced it.

- In identifying a potential problem, ensure that it is big, unique, valuable, and timely.

TARGET THE RIGHT CUSTOMER

Chapter 2

CUSTOMER SEGMENTATION

"You need to be so specific in your
customer segmentation, it hurts."

—Mike Wien
Author of The Specific Edge

In creating your Business Model Canvas (BMC), it is critical to focus on the right customers. Look back at the BMC and you'll see this is the second step. The simple reason is time and money are finite, so you will need to properly identify the right customers who will value and buy your products and/or services.

Many of my clients are cautious about being too targeted because they feel they may be losing opportunities and leaving money on the table. They say, "Companies like Amazon do everything, so why can't we?" The simple answer is Amazon started in a very specific niche as an online book seller and only *grew carefully* after executives researched and tested other opportunities. And, by the way, you aren't Amazon, which is a unicorn among unicorns.

As a result, if you overreach, more than likely you'll have less impact and dilute your offering.

To avoid this happening, you should create customer segmentation that shows users and uses for the types of services and products you wish to provide. Segmentation allows you to divide a market's customers into subgroups in a way that optimizes your company's ability to profit from the fact that customers have different needs, priorities, and economic levers.

For a business-to-business opportunity, executives typically start segmenting customers by industries/vertical markets and company size.

INDUSTRY ANALYSIS

To improve your ability to segment your prospects and customers, you should start with an analysis of your particular industry, including data on the profitability of existing market leaders as well as researching technology changes, channel changes, and current and potential competitors. Consider a source such as the MoneyTree Report (www.pwcmoneytree.com) to uncover angel and venture financing in a sector.

Once you've done your research, the next step is to score the data and categorize the elements to determine if you should take the next step. Use Figure 2-1, Factors to Consider, which includes the characteristics to help you make an honest assessment about each one. The scoring key is 1 to 10, with 10 being the highest score and an ideal setup for venture success. If the factors are conducive to a new venture, score a 7; score a 5 if they are neither a barrier nor a support for success. Finally, a 3 indicates you would face a significant challenge, and a 1 is a potential showstopper for a new venture. The highest score is 100, and any industry scoring over 75 is worth considering. Conversely, a score of 25 or lower should be avoided. If you land in the midrange, consider how you would be able to overcome industry obstacles. Additionally, if you end up with a low score, consider looking at a different industry or another segment of the industry.

Customer Segment Factors to Consider

	Facts/Data about Your Target Industry	Industry Score (1–10)
Current industry segment/niche size		
Industry segment/niche growth rate		
Favorable trends sweeping across the industry		
Fragmented competition		
Feasible, money-making model in the industry		
Activity in start-ups, financing, and deals in the segment/niche		
Industry life cycle stage (not too early or too late)		
Existing distribution channels		
Reasonably priced, widely available components, technologies, and ingredients		
No barriers to entry in terms of capital, production, and distribution		
Total Score:		

Figure 2-1

USER ANALYSIS

With internet access and social media, we can do more research with more reach.

One methodology is joining a Facebook group that is specific to your potential customer segment.

As an example, there is a group called Worldwide Renewable Energy Professionals. If you want to start or expand in this industry and are trying to evaluate the opportunity, this is a great group to join.

Ultimately, you want to rank the customer segment factors and determine if the score provides a strong opportunity.

Time to pause and put what you learned to work.

Find a Facebook group where your potential customer may participate, including providing and seeking information.

PRO POINTERS

- It is critical to find the right customers, and that is the second step of the BMC. It may seem counterintuitive; however, the more tightly you segment your customers, the better your chance for success.

- Simply, you can't be all things to all people. Amazon did not start out as it exists today.

- Industry analysis is as important as customer segmentation. Score your industry honestly or you will only be fooling yourself.

- Conduct a user analysis to gauge demand. Facebook groups is a good starting point.

Chapter 3

MARKET RESEARCH

"Without data, you're just another
person with an opinion."

—*W. Edwards Deming*
Engineer, Statistician, Author,
and Management Consultant

In accurately creating your Business Model Canvas (BMC), you've clearly defined the problem first and have developed the solution only after you identified your target customers and developed a unique value proposition. Only then is it time for you to develop your solution.

Of course, you're passionate about your solution—or why else would you have launched a business around it! Passion can go a long way, but I must caution you not to let that passion lead you to be overly zealous. Being too in love with your idea and solution can blind you to obvious flaws and growth limitations, and it can alter your good business judgment.

Before going forward, you must take some time to be your ideas' and company's biggest critic. Beyond doing the typical SWOT (strengths, weaknesses, opportunities, threats) assessment, you actually should try to tear down your own business, zeroing in on the cracks and flaws in your business and its foundation. You can also contact a mentor or trusted advisor to objectively coach you throughout this process. This approach will help you more clearly see the weaknesses in your proposed solution and organization. Many entrepreneurs only focus on the positives of their idea—how great it will be and how well they are going to execute on it with their unique approach and skill set. I'm not suggesting that you shouldn't move forward with passion, but you should do so after you've tested to ensure the problem your idea solves actually exists. I am cautioning you that too much passion can lead you to crash and burn when you fail to uncover the flaws and then fix them before they become fatal.

> **Don't only focus on the positives of your idea. In addition to doing market research, look for reasons your business could fail. Ask a trusted mentor or colleague for flaws in your business plan.**

Approach your business as any good investor would. Investors will always first look for the weaknesses, asking if the business is defensible and then scalable. Investors are interested in growth, and if you want to grow your business, you must take this same approach. If you have already determined the holes in your business and developed patches for those holes, you will be more attractive to investors when you approach them and your company will be better positioned for greater growth.

Being too headstrong and refusing to pivot when necessary can cost you your business.

WHO NEEDS IT?

As you'll recall, the second step in a well-crafted BMC is the target audience. Who has the problem you are going to solve? What really is the market opportunity? Even if you've developed the absolute ideal solution and you are the only one on the planet who can deliver it, if only a handful of prospects have the problem, you will never grow your business. It's common sense.

Market intelligence, including size, segmentation, and forecast opportunity, can be used to inform and assess:

- New market entry
- Geographic expansion
- New product development
- M&A due diligence
- Large-scale capital investment
- General strategic planning

In conducting market research, you will want to consider several questions, as outlined in Figure 3-1.

Key Questions

Industry Size	How big is the industry? If your solution is already covering a large percentage of prospects, there is little or no room for growth.
Growth	How fast is the industry growing? Has it reached its peak so companies serving the industry are commoditized?
Competition	How many competitors are there and how big are they?
Funding	How much better are your competitors capitalized?
Opportunity	Is there whitespace in the industry? This is unmet and unarticulated needs that create innovation opportunities.

Figure 3-1

Ideally, you should conduct your market research before launching. Whether or not you've done that initially, if you are struggling to grow or are considering additional or different or expanded products or services, now is the time.

There are two different types of market research, primary and secondary. Primary research is secured directly through prospective buyer interaction. Secondary feedback is based on available research on the industry, its products, and its services. Figure 3-2, Market Research Data, indicates various types of data that can inform your business.

Market Research Data

Primary Data	Secondary Data
Interviews	Market Research Reports
Surveys	Industry Associations
Focus Groups	Trade Associations
Social Media Monitoring	Company Websites
	Government Statistics
	Google/Search Engines

Figure 3-2

At USI, we met with corporate leaders who said they were struggling with the recent recession and were therefore thinking about outsourcing noncore functions, including corporate real estate. *Boom!* That was great primary research.

When I wanted to start a consulting practice for commercial real estate service firms, I discovered a problem when I directly observed a number of small and mid-sized firms in the industry that had plateaued and were struggling to grow. I also met with trade organization leadership and confirmed there was opportunity for a solution to this problem. Finally, I searched a number of key words associated with real estate services consulting and didn't find an extensive list. Midcourse Advisors was launched after this market analysis was completed. I've since expanded into the B2B services space, but only after I launched successfully with a defined niche.

Nothing can substitute for primary data, but if you want to get a high-level view of an industry that you may be interested in entering or expanding into, secondary data is a strong place to start. You just need to understand that secondary data may be outdated, is already evident to your competition, and may not be specific enough for your potential application. Nevertheless, you can gain this information quickly and inexpensively. If the opportunity is there, you can refine it with more extensive primary data. You can go to www.marketresearch.com for resources for secondary data.

Whether you're just starting a business or seeking to grow an established one, solid market research will uncover your customer preferences and how to deliver on them, identify and monitor your competition, mitigate risk, and reveal revenue and profit growth opportunities. Market research findings help you drive other facets of your business, including sales potential, new customer attraction, and retention for repeat and referral business.

Primary research can be further divided into quantitative and qualitative methods.

Quantitative market research collects numerical data after statistical analysis to uncover and understand trends. It more easily allows for comparisons and contrasts. Based on standardized questions and surveys, it is often a more structured approach. However, to get the clearest picture (as with any survey), you need a large number of respondents, and those respondents must closely mirror your desired target audience.

You can conduct surveys in a number of ways, including face-to-face

Much of your primary research should have been covered when you were creating your BMC by getting detailed answers about:

- Who are my customers and how do I reach them?

- What solutions do buyers need or want?

- What factors influence buying decisions?

- What prices should I set?

- Who are my competitors and what are their strengths and weaknesses?

> Don't overlook free information that is available from local and national resources, including the government, business organizations, industry groups, etc. Some data may not be current, but much of it will be useful.

interviews, phone, email, snail mail, and online/web forms. No matter how you conduct a market research survey, you must keep it short and simple, easy to read, and move from general to specific questions without asking leading questions.

Qualitative market research is the information derived from a less structured approach. Think "discuss" rather than "answer a question" to better understand the difference between qualitative and quantitative methods. Focus groups, in-depth interviews and your own observations are some of the approaches to gathering qualitative data and information.

Secondary research is that which is already done for you. Although it may not be as targeted to your specific business, it can provide valuable information. It uses outside information gathered from government agencies, industry and trade associations, media sources, business organizations, educational institutions, etc.

Free public sources (e.g. government, public libraries, etc.) can help you uncover information about population trends, industrial development, and local and regional demographic information. Though you usually have to pay a fee to join a trade association or chamber of commerce, these organizations can provide thorough, accurate information about your industry and the geographic region. Local media also maintains a wealth of demographic information for their own sales departments and may be quite willing to share that in their media kits. Finally, don't overlook educational institutions that are often conducting research into myriad topics. This includes many healthcare initiatives as well as use of artificial intelligence and big data.

MARKET RESEARCH AND MARKETING

Both your quantitative and qualitative research should reveal not only what your customers want, but *how* they want to receive information about it. This is where the concept of building an omnichannel business comes into play.

Consider a retail business. It likely has a brick-and-mortar store, a website, a social media platform, a catalog, and an app. Historically, when alternate channels evolved with the digital age, they often competed with each other as well as traditional sales outlets. The business landscape was filled with siloes with little collaboration.

With solid market research—including your own primary research to determine how and when customers want to be reached—you can now take an omnichannel approach that blends various means together based on data collection. The same channels still exist, but now they work in concert with each other with the customer at the center of all decisions. Whatever the customers want—however they choose to engage with you—is what they get.

Keep in mind that multichannel and omnichannel are not the same thing. Not all multichannel approaches are omnichannel. In thinking about the retail business in the earlier example, it was multichannel; it had a store, a website, an app, and a catalog. However, unless they are integrated, seamless, and cohesive, the customer experience will not be an omnichannel one. You must give customers what they want, the way they want it, and when they want it, all in a personalized way. And you must track their activity and collect data points to use for their future interactions.

Disney provides a great example of an omnichannel experience. First, its fantastic website is mobile responsive, even its trip-planning segment. Once you book, you can use the My Disney Experience tool to plan your trip from dining to securing Fast Passes. Use the mobile app in the parks to find the attractions you want to see along with real-time estimated wait times. Finally, its Magic Band program is your hotel room key, photo storage for all of your pictures, and a food-ordering tool. Omnichannel indeed!

RESEARCH RESULTS

Ideally, your research will support your solution and reveal that you have a great idea for a viable, scalable business that will grow as you envision. That said, it may also reveal your current limitations for that growth and where you may be lacking in certain skill sets and expertise. This may include your own skill set.

For example, you may be a great technologist who has developed a killer software solution that people will beat a path to your door to acquire . . . but you don't know the first thing about running a business or sales and marketing. You might have a great executive background but limited knowledge of operations and production.

Market research may even lead to the conclusion that you are not the best leader for the business. Leverage your own skills, as they can best enable your company for growth. Be open to building out your team and putting the best people in the positions most suited for their skills. As a smart entrepreneur, your greatest interest should be in your equity returns as opposed to the title listed on your business card.

Know when to listen to mentors. Depending on your own skill set, you might be able to effectively conduct your own market research. However, many entrepreneurs with great solutions do not understand how to conduct market research or even build a sound business plan that addresses the right concerns—those that will attract investors and enable sustainable growth.

You will find that the ROI for engaging a business consultant pays off handsomely.

PRO POINTERS

- There's a line between being passionate about your solution and being overly zealous. Crossing that line can blind you to flaws and growth limitations.

- The best solution will never get off the ground if there is no market for the problem it solves.

- Always address the following issues as part of your market research: industry size, industry growth potential, competition, funding, and opportunity.

- Market research comprises both primary and secondary research, and as part of primary research, you must gather both quantitative and qualitative data.

- Your research results should uncover not only what your customers want, but how they want to receive information about it. Once you know that, you can more effectively create an omnichannel approach. Be open to building out your team and putting the best people in the positions most suited for their skills and how they best work in an omnichannel market.

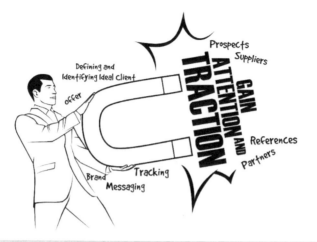

Prospects
Suppliers
Defining and
Identifying Ideal Client
offer
GAIN
ATTENTION AND
TRACTION
References
Partners
Brand
Messaging
Tracking

LAUNCH PROFITABLY

Chapter 4

GAIN ATTENTION AND TRACTION

"The ones who are crazy enough to
think they can change the world are
the ones that do. Think different."

—Steve Jobs
Founder of Apple

In 1984, Apple got a lot of attention for its Macintosh personal computer by airing a gripping commercial during that year's Super Bowl.

Through a dystopian lens, the ad demonstrated how IBM wanted to dominate and control the future and that Apple's new product was the way to stop IBM's dominance. Apple wanted something that would have millions of people thinking about computers, specifically the Macintosh. Well, this advertising certainly worked.

In fact, the commercial was so groundbreaking, it set the stage for Apple's growth that we know so well today.

Once you've clearly defined the problem and launched your solution, to grow like an Inc. 500 company, you must gain traction quickly by adding customers beyond those you first identified in the BMC process. The beauty of gaining traction is that once it begins, it can be self-perpetuating. However, you will never gain traction unless you first gain attention.

Gary Vaynerchuk, CEO of Vayner Media and well-known social media guru, has called "attention" the new currency of business.[1] Before you can tell others about your product and service and how it can solve their problems, you need to gain attention. It is no longer good enough to have great content if no one sees it, hears it, or feels it.

The new currency of business is ATTENTION.

Why is gaining attention so hard? The amount of information and the number of channels through which we are exposed to such information keeps growing and growing . . . and growing. We are constantly inundated with messages competing for our attention, which means we have trouble focusing on the ones most important.

In fact, Forbes reported in 2019 that more than 90 percent of the world's data was generated in only the past two years.[2] There are 2.5 quintillion bytes of data created each day at our current pace, but that pace is only accelerating with the growth of the Internet of Things (IoT). Since then, the amount of data generated as continued to grow exponentially.

So, how can you gain attention? According to Ben Parr, author of the book *Captivology*, people are always looking for quick and easy indicators for quality. This makes it hard to break into the game, but easier to stay on top once you're there. Parr also suggests the more people are curious about what will happen next, the stronger the attention it generates and the more people will remember it.

My view is that you need to demonstrate quality and how you

---

1 Gary Vaynerchuk, "Don't Take Attention for Granted!" GaryVaynerchuk.com, 2017, https://www.garyvaynerchuk.com/taking-attention-granted/.

2 Bernard Marr, "How Much Data Do We Create Every Day? The Mind-Blowing Stats Everyone Should Read," Forbes, May 21, 2018, https://www.forbes.com/sites/bernardmarr/2018/05/21/how-much-data-do-we-create-every-day-the-mind-blowing-stats-everyone-should-read/#5d7bdccf60ba.

differentiate yourself in providing that quality. Then, you need to lead your prospects on a journey to solve their problems.

For example, a service business may deliver results faster, enabling its customers to enjoy the benefits sooner. For a product business, a quality assurance program may inspire confidence that the product will work according to specifications.

You need to put out relevant content that will both educate and influence your prospects and customers. As an example, if you are a SaaS company with a great technology product that provides healthcare management for diabetics, you could write an article/blog about how technology can help diabetics manage their insulin intake. You would post this on your company's website and other social media platforms. Then, using Google ads, Facebook ads, and LinkedIn, you would advertise to a targeted market for diabetics. It would link to your company's website, where they would find the article, and then, we have attention.

As I'm writing this book, Instagram, Twitter, and LinkedIn are the most scalable social media tools to reach people and gain attention. Facebook is the largest, but it is facing public pressure on a number of fronts. Emails, getting a phone call, or watching a TV commercial aren't the only channels that work to get attention today.

Clients often ask me, "What are some of the best elements that can make you different and gain attention?" It is easier said than done, but, based on Figure 4-1, it is about creating a better mousetrap and then being able to communicate it well.

Elements to Gain Attention

Element	Value	Example
Convenience	Time saver	Uber
Reliability/Dependability	Consistent outcomes	McDonald's
Quality	Performance based on engineering	BMW
Customer Service	Pleasant experience	Chick-fil-A
Innovation	Newest technology	Apple
Creativity	Ability to inspire	Disney

Figure 4-1

Notice I did not mention price. If prospective clients are evaluating you and your company based on price, you are a commodity and will never be valued as highly.

It is important to note not every potential customer will be ready to consume your service or product when you want to deliver it based on their budget availability, resource constraints, and other projects competing for dollars and consideration.

THE ELEVATOR PITCH

I'm sure you've probably heard of an elevator pitch. It simply means describing your product and/or service to someone succinctly enough that you can get his attention in the time an elevator takes the person to his/her floor. The pitch can be used at meetings, parties, and other venues. The key is not to waste time to get your value proposition across, as time is limited.

But what is in an elevator pitch and what makes it effective?

Whether you are leading a new or established business, the Statement of Venture Concept is something you can either tell prospective customers or have them read in fewer than thirty seconds, understand, and be ready to ask some questions about.

This statement has a specific structure that focuses on the target customer, the problem to be solved, the unique differences from other competitive offerings, and the benefits customers will expect. The format is as follows:

> ACME is our business that *solves what problem* for *which target customers*. We are unique because of *why customers buy*. The benefits we expect to provide include *A, B, and C.*

As an example, at USI, our Statement of Venture Concept was:

> USI is a business that makes commercial real estate a competitive advantage for corporate occupiers. We are unique in that we only represent tenants and offer a fully integrated suite of services that allows

us to provide expertise, objectivity, and flexibility at less cost than corporations can provide themselves. We save our customers millions of dollars each year while aligning real estate and operational needs.

> **Don't overlook your elevator pitch. This powerful statement is how you will attract and keep customers. Work on creating a powerful description of your business and practice it before you deliver it.**

Write and practice articulating your Statement of Venture Concept. It will help you focus on your offering and also how well you communicate it.

I incorporated the above recommended methodologies in this section, but I also went further to gain attention. Most of my success came from patience and persistence. Certainly, if all the ducks lined up, the cycle time was shorter and the sale was easier, but that is not the norm for almost any business with any complex sale.

I took a longer-term view in my stance and communications. This meant that I didn't behave like a car salesperson at the end of the month pushing to make that month's quota. Instead, I demonstrated I was ready and capable when the clients were.

One notable success involved Sonoco, a paper products manufacturer and distributor based in South Carolina. I knew this company was a good candidate for USI's services because it didn't have enough resources or a process to optimize its real estate. Sonoco had an existing local provider who wasn't very capable, but had a strong, long-term relationship with some of Sonoco's senior management. I stayed in touch with the real estate director, who liked us but didn't have the clout to make a change. I kept abreast of the firm's industry and sent articles and information about managing real estate more productively, whether it was related to USI's services or not. We called these "Smart Bombs." When in the area, I made sure to meet with him for coffee. When doing so, I didn't sell and he wasn't ready to buy.

Well, about three years later, Sonoco had a reorganization, and some of the senior management team, including those who had the relationship with the local provider, left. Within a week, I received a call from my point contact at Sonoco, and we were hired shortly thereafter.

Finally, it pays to think outside the box and be creative. There is a company in the Atlanta area called Hot Schedules. This firm provides software and service to the restaurant industry to help operators schedule and manage better. The firm was seeking to scale properly as its business was growing. To get the senior executives' attention, I created a menu (as you would get at a restaurant), indicating the choices the firm would need to make to scale properly. The menu is shown in Figure 4-2.

Scaling Menu

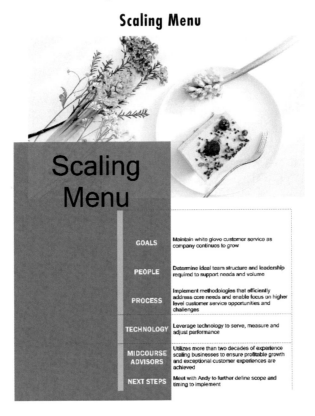

Figure 4-2

Today, it is far easier to gain attention through social media, which is addressed in more detail in Chapter 9. However, it doesn't need to be a big effort to generate dividends. What is important is content quality and consistency.

For example, there is a real estate brokerage firm in Louisiana called Elfin Realty. This company posts video content (vlogs) on Facebook, LinkedIn, and other sites almost daily. Rather than having a big studio with production teams, Elfin simply turns on the camera when employees identify something during their business day that they think may be valuable to their customers and prospects.

They recently had to engage an appraiser for the sale of a building for a client, so they quickly and easily created a video about how to evaluate and engage an appraiser. You can do this too.

TO ACT OR NOT TO ACT

It is important to prioritize based on both feasibility and benefit. Tasks that are easiest to implement and achieve a material impact should always be addressed first. Figure 4-3, Feasibility and Benefit, shows the factors when managing a sales team, but the same thinking and approach can be applied to your efforts to gain attention and traction.

Feasibility and Benefit

Figure 4-3

When you are putting out fires, you may lose sight of the feasibility and benefit for the project you're pursuing. It's important to take time to assess the impact of failing to act. In the case of gaining attention and traction, is it hundreds of prospects you're either missing or have the opportunity to attract? Is there a better ROI on a certain approach or social media platform? Can you get to market sooner?

In addition to acting (or not acting) at the right time, honesty is always important. Don't ever sell what you and your team can't deliver, because your credibility will be irreparably harmed. However, leaning forward a bit works well. This means you have the capability to solve a problem similar to what you have solved. Be transparent, but not afraid to propose if it makes sense for you and your prospective customer. Then, you'll be paid for your solution and the problems you can solve and pain you can alleviate.

For prospects who aren't responding, I frequently send them a proposal. It may not contain all the information to address all their needs with 100 percent accuracy, but that's not the point. The point is that I'm demonstrating the thinking and process I use to add value. If it delivers value and demonstrates impactful results, I can typically generate a conversation that then leads to an opportunity. It's a solid approach to gaining attention.

DISCOVERY OFFER

Sometimes, for whatever reason, even if you've taken all the right actions to generate attention and draw a prospect to a decision, the prospective client simply may not be ready to move forward. One way to overcome the indecision is to provide a discovery offer or the Good/Better/Best approach. The "good" is your initial discovery offer—that which the prospect buys with a lower cost of entry that gives you the opportunity to get in the door to prove value and then expand the scope of what you can offer, moving the client up to more expensive offerings.

It's important to keep in mind that you don't need to reinvent the wheel to offer higher-level and premium versions of your product or service. For example, consider the Lexus. It's built on Toyota's Camry chassis, so there's no manufacturing overhaul needed to produce a car with the added features and bells and whistles that consumers want and for which they're willing to pay.

Let's say you manufacture scarves. You already have the loom and equipment in place, and you have your entry-level product. You can easily upgrade your offering to the "better" and "best" categories simply by improving the quality of the yarn.

You gain attention and traction by providing more than one flavor, but you must create your Good/Better/Best platform in such a way that the latter offerings are not completely disparate. Employ the concept of modularity by always starting with the same base model.

Good, Better, Best

Good	Better	Best
Feature 1	Feature 1	Feature 1
Feature 2	Feature 2	Feature 2
	Feature 3	Feature 3
		Feature 4

Figure 4-4

ASSIGNMENT Time to pause and put what you learned to work.

List your services and determine which are Good/Better/Best.

PERSONAL CONNECTION

When it comes to gaining attention, there is often too much reliance on emails, texting, social media messaging, and other forms of "silent" communication. While they have a place, they often diminish the ability to really connect authentically and fully.

As Waldo Waldman, motivational speaker, author, and military veteran, has pointed out in one of his "Fly with Waldo" blogs, "In combat, fighter pilots minimize radio communication to prevent information from being intercepted by the enemy. Instead, we used hand signals and flight maneuvers. However, during emergencies, unsafe situations, or in the heat of battle, we throw all that aside and get on the radio to help our wingmen take action. . . . Verbal communication does more than just pass on information. It can relay emotion and impact one's engagement with others."[3]

Pick up the phone and make a call. Share an introduction or give a referral. Ask how you can help with a problem. It will make a real difference in your ability to build trust and create a relationship. It's a great way to gain attention and traction and grow your sales and your business as a result. As Waldo shared, "A few years back, I went to a sales conference and the number-one performing salesman said the key to his success was exactly this. He picked up the phone, he built relationships, he nurtured his prospects and clients, and let them know with his heart and his voice that he wanted their business and would do everything he could to earn it and keep it."

THE LAW OF DIFFUSION OF INNOVATION

Once you have gotten someone's attention, to effectively gain traction in getting more business or keeping that person as a customer, you must understand the Law of Diffusion of Innovation. This is a theory that examines how, why, and at what rate new ideas and technology spread and are accepted. First popularized in the 1962 book *Diffusion of Innovations*, by Everett Rogers, the theory holds that four main elements influence the spread of a new idea: the innovation itself, communication channels, time, and a social system. In today's marketplace, the internet and social media obviously provide the channels and social system, and technology allows for a great deal of speed and time compression. With the right idea, product, and/or service and its adoption, it can easily become self-sustaining, practically guaranteeing continuous traction.

---

3   Waldo Waldman, "Pick Up the Phone – How to Create Connection with Conversation," Your Wingman, visited April 13, 2020, https://www.yourwingman.com/pick-up-the-phone/.

New Product Tipping Point

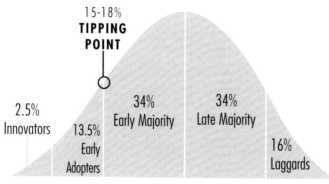

15-18%
TIPPING POINT

2.5% Innovators

13.5% Early Adopters

34% Early Majority

34% Late Majority

16% Laggards

Figure 4-5

The theory is represented by a typical bell curve, starting with the innovators and ending with the laggards:

The innovators and early adopters are quick to embrace new ideas and technology and have no fear of being on the "bleeding" edge, where they may jump at something that ultimately fails. The early majority, on the other hand, want someone else to lead the way before they'll sign on. They're not willing to be on the bleeding edge but like to think they're still on the leading edge. The late majority needs still more proof that an idea or innovation is worth their investment, and the laggards usually have to be dragged kicking and screaming to try something new.

The Law of Diffusion of Innovation indicates that mass market success—a.k.a. traction—of an idea or innovation will only occur once you've reached the tipping point, which typically occurs at about 15 to 18 percent of market penetration. For your particular and specific market identified, to gain traction, you must reach the early majority audience, but they aren't willing to try something until someone else has tried it first, so they can see that it works and that they aren't at risk of wasting time and money.

The early majority is pragmatic and looks to the innovators and early adopters to lead the way. These folks are the ones comfortable trying anything new, no matter the expense. Waiting in line overnight to be the first in the store to purchase the latest iPhone is an example of an innovator or early adopter. Apple certainly has its share of innovators and early adopters. The early majority waits a few weeks and walks in and simply buys it off the shelf, and if the item is on backorder, they'll have to wait some more. They're fine with that possibility.

Where anyone falls on the scale is a matter of self-perception. The innovators make decisions about what they believe about the world and their place in it, not the specific product or service. Innovators and early adopters make purchases for themselves; they buy based on how the product makes them feel more so than for the technology. They revel in being first and want others to see them as being first. The early majority sees themselves as the pragmatists, not willing to spend money or time unless a product or service has proven itself to be valuable. They also want greater reassurance that it won't fail.

CROSSING THE CHASM

Being first obviously isn't important to the early majority, but they do represent the point of critical mass, which is why reaching the tipping point is an important milestone to gaining traction. While companies can achieve a 10 percent conversion rate on new business, that won't enable your business to sustain itself, much less grow. As a result, you need to find more innovators and early adopters because the tipping point still remains at least five percentage points away.

This gap is referred to as the chasm, and crossing the chasm is a concept introduced by Geoffrey Moore in his book *Crossing the Chasm: Marketing and Selling High-Tech Products to Mainstream Customers*. As it turns out, getting the early majority into the game is challenging, and you need those pragmatists in order to cross the tipping point.

Keep in mind you don't need the entire universe of early adopters; you need a small percentage that will allow you to reach the tipping point to move the needle in your favor and gain mass market acceptance. The pragmatists will not move until they're under duress with a pain point. People in pain from this group will be the ones who move first. You can reach them by focusing on case studies and early use cases that prove you have the solution to the pain they're experiencing.

Ideally focus on one very successful use case and find a niche market with a problem best addressed with your solution and not solvable by conventional methods. The clients you want to focus on to cross the chasm won't be in exploration mode—they should be desperate, needing your solution right now.

REAL-WORLD EXAMPLES

At USI, we gained traction by demonstrating how an alliance creates far more value than a typical one-off brokerage transactional model.

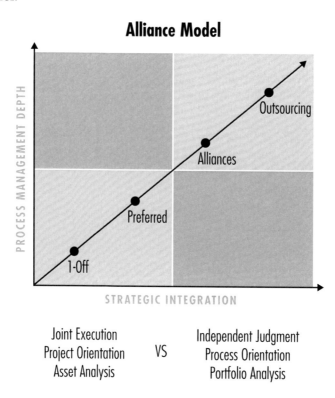

Alliance Model

Figure 4-6

This innovative model got the attention of the C-suite, especially the CFO, where they recognized we offered objectivity, expertise, and flexibility, all at a cost less than they could staff themselves.

Of particular note was how we articulated and demonstrated that real estate was often one of a company's highest costs (outside of staffing, manufacturing, and R&D) and that our platform would actually impact Earnings Per Share (EPS). Figure 4-7 demonstrates a material impact based on our proposed value proposition.

Earnings Per Share Impact

	AVERAGE ANNUAL ESTIMATED EPS IMPACT	AGGREGATE ESTIMATED EPS IMPACT
Net Savings Benefit	$8,888,813	$44,444,065
Estimated Effective Tax Rate	39.00%	39.00%
Tax Effect	($3,466,637)	($17,333,185)
After Tax Savings	$5,422,176	$27,110,880
Shares Outstanding	260,172,260	260,172,260
Impact to EPS	$0.0208	$0.1042
Current Earning per Share	$2.48	$2.48
Market Capitalization	$8,760,000,000	$8,760,000,000
Current Price per Share	$33.67	$33.67

Figure 4-7

At IEM, we demonstrated how we could reduce cost and help clients achieve their corporate sustainability goals. This positively impacted their financials and their company brand.

Efficiency Optimization

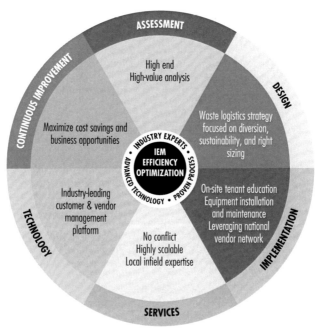

Figure 4-8

Customer Value vs. Asset Base

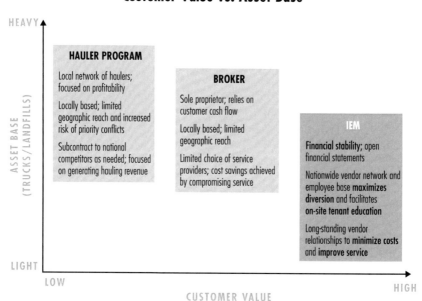

Figure 4-9

At both USI and IEM, we were an unknown brand to certain prospective customers, so we needed to be more creative to get their attention. Ideally, once we got attention, we'd receive specifics about their problems and be able to craft a detailed solution. In absence of attention, we would do some research on the company and send a high-level proposal demonstrating our unique value proposition and how we could address their problem(s). It would incorporate a number of assumptions, which were clearly identified. When we did this, we frequently accomplished what we called "snapping their heads back" because it clearly stood out got their attention. From there, we would often be welcomed to meet and take a deeper dive to provide a more detailed proposal.

Once you gain attention and start to move a few of these pragmatists toward your solution, you can reach the tipping point. At the tipping point, the early majority now gets the sense that "everyone's doing this" and greater numbers self-propel themselves toward your innovation. Ah, traction.

PRO POINTERS

- You must first gain attention before you can demonstrate how well your product and service can solve a prospect's problem.

- Your Statement of Venture Concept (a.k.a. your elevator pitch) must succinctly explain what problem you solve, for whom, why customers buy, and the benefits you provide.

- Gain attention by building a better mousetrap and communicate it well, addressing the elements of convenience, reliability, quality, customer service, innovation, and creativity.

- Many times, patience and persistence pay off handsomely when trying to gain attention.

- Provide a discovery offer and make it part of your Good/Better/Best platform. You can escalate offerings without having to recreate from scratch.

- Never overlook the power of personal connection. You can generate a lot of attention (and sales!) by picking up the phone and having a conversation.

- The Law of Diffusion of Innovation is represented by a bell curve, with the innovators on one side and the laggards at the other end of the scale.

- Traction occurs when you reach the tipping point—15–18 percent of market penetration.

- Where anyone falls on the curve depends on self-perception. Innovators make purchases based on how it makes them feel rather than the product or service itself.

- There is a gap, "the chasm," that exists between the innovators and early adopters and the tipping point. Crossing the chasm is essential to mass market adoption.

- To move toward mass market acceptance, target those in the early majority who are under duress and experiencing the very pain you solve.

- Use creativity to gain clients' attention and "snap their heads back."

Chapter 5

LEVERAGE SUCCESSES

"It is much easier to put existing
resources to better use than to develop
resources where they do not exist."

—*George Soros*
Investor and Philanthropist

Hand in hand with gaining traction is your ability to leverage the successes you have already had in order to grow your business. You may have a rock star sales team working for you, but no matter how good they may be, they will never be your best salespeople. Your customers—your happy, over-the-top-thrilled-with-your-service customers—are truly your best salespeople.

Making your customers happy should be a priority every day. This is because the three easiest sales you will ever make include:

1. Repeat sale of the same product/service to a happy customer
2. Expanded product/service offering to that same customer

3. Sale to a prospect who's been referred by a happy customer

Existing happy customers are also a good testing ground for new products or services.

Regarding referrals, it helps to know why your client would provide a reference in the first place. It's almost always for one of these reasons:

1. They love your company, the product and service, and the people who work there and want to see you succeed.
2. They get to expand their network and meet interesting people who can help them.
3. They get special treatment plus the opportunity to promote themselves and their successes with your company or product to a peer.

Once you understand which one of these motivates any one of your customers, it's a lot easier to ask for their participation.

Tactically, I suggest setting expectations at the beginning regarding work flow, communications, touch points, and deadlines as well as the end result—your solution—and your customers will be happy to be your biggest advocate. Define what the ROI will be for your client at the start and then exceed that.

A key part of setting the expectation at the start is to have it work both ways to allow you to leverage your efforts and success. "Here's what we'll deliver to you, the time frame for delivery, and what you can expect. I know we'll exceed those expectations, and when we do, I expect you to be an advocate for us."

> Use specific language in setting client expectations. Spell out what you will deliver, the time frame, and what the client can expect. Exceed those expectations and your client will be your greatest salesperson.

Set that up from the start; however, you have to go a bit further and do some of the referral/advocacy legwork for them. You probably already know that the easiest way to get a referral is to actually write the letter on behalf of the person referring you and then simply forward it for their review and signature. That's a very simple example. I suggest that you take it much further.

REAL-WORLD EXAMPLES

We handled customer advocacy very effectively at both USI and IEM. First, we assured the customer that we would absolutely solve their pressing problems and save them quite a lot of money in the process. Then, we were clear about what their ROI would be and how we would be measured. Next, we said we wanted them to be our biggest advocate when we delivered as promised and even exceeded their expectations. Part of that advocacy was having them appear in print ads and video testimonials that we would develop and fund. Often, this was written into our agreements with our clients.

For example, United Technologies was one of USI's biggest customers. We promised to save the company $42 million over twenty-four months and went into the relationship with the understanding from the outset that upon completion, we'd feature United Technologies' senior real estate executive, Ron Zappile, in an ad in *CFO Magazine*. Of course, he was thrilled with the publicity for him and his company in addition to saving $90 million, far greater than expected. It was the proverbial win-win. The ad copy underscored the terrific benefit of the relationship between both organizations. USI gained a true advocate for prospects and future sales, and United Technologies gained no-cost exposure that the manufacturer would not have received otherwise.

Client Testimonial

A Partnership
that has saved
$90 Million

United
Technologies

Ron Zappile
President
United Technologies Realty, Inc.

"PARTNERING WITH USI HAS RESULTED IN IMPROVED EFFICIENCIES
AND GREATER STRATEGIC VALUE—HELPING UNITED TECHNOLOGIES TO STAY COMPETITIVE"

Figure 5-1

This is just one example to get you thinking about what you can do to leverage success, especially with your early customers. Another step we took was to actually include language in the contract regarding how referrals and post-project advocacy would be handled upon completion when we far exceeded their expectations. "If we exceed XYZ metrics, we expect you to be a great reference for us by providing the following . . ."

Another tool is the Customer Success Scorecard, which will be explained in depth in Chapter 13. In short, the tool allows us to set clear expectations up front and encourages customers to rate us throughout the process and project rather than waiting until the end to provide feedback about our performance.

Don't hesitate to ask existing customers for references to new prospective customers. You can set up a tour or have a dinner, where your advocate and the prospective customer can meet, and you can coach and orchestrate the conversation.

Don't hesitate to ask customers if they know people who could benefit from your products/services and ask them to make a personal introduction.

Check on customers' LinkedIn profiles to see who they know and request introductions directly.

Overinvest in client setup/launches to establish credibility and set the right tone from the outset.

Lastly, to minimize risk and maximize return, grow with your client. If you and your company have been a quality partner, your client would be smart to engage with you first as they expand their services/products. At both USI and IEM, we did this very successfully. Within five years at both companies, we operated in virtually every state across the country. At USI, our model was to operate on-site at our clients' locations, so we almost universally only expanded where clients had additional needs with locations we could occupy.

Consider the following approaches for creating and partnering with clients who will advocate for your company:

1. Recorded and written materials

These reusable assets include:

- Permission to use clients' names/logos/images in marketing communications
- Written testimonials and quotes for general publication
- Agreement to be quoted in a press release and case studies with named clients
- Archived recorded webinars
- Taped audio and/or video testimonials
- Taped third-party, in-depth interviews to be

revealed with permission during the discovery process, sometimes in lieu of a one-on-one conversation with a prospect

2. Clients who will make live, mass audience presentations

Generally, these are not reusable. A client may agree to do a few presentations that can reach a fairly large audience.

- Agree to be interviewed by journalists and/or analysts who will distribute the information to others
- Sit on a panel at a trade show
- Attend a prospect networking event (breakfast or other smaller high-level gathering)
- Speeches at trade shows or webinars

3. Clients who will speak and meet one on one with prospects

Again, these are not reusable, so they are generally reserved for special occasions, helping to land the most important prospects. Unfortunately, your sales team will probably want to use them like crazy!

- Agree to speak on the phone with individual prospects (serving as a reference)
- Allow prospects to visit in person for a tour

ASSIGNMENT

Time to pause and put what you learned to work.

Make a list of clients and other relationships you can leverage. Determine which ones you can leverage directly and make contact.

DIFFERENTIATE YOURSELF

As you gain success and begin stacking up happy customers, be certain you use that experience and expertise as a differentiator to continue to set yourself apart from your competitors. This is how you boost your unfair advantage—that which competitors cannot copy and prospects cannot purchase elsewhere.

I recently worked with a client, ICON Commercial, an established team of real estate generalists who wanted to grow their business faster. They knew that serving growing technology companies was key to their growth but they needed help, so they turned to my team and I at Midcourse Advisors. The following Figure 5-2 shows the process that I used to help ICON differentiate and create its unfair advantage:

Differentiation Approach

Approach	Description
Online Presence	Updated their LinkedIn profiles to position themselves as the real estate expert for growing technology companies
Target Market	Helped them focus on growing technology companies that were leaving the incubator space to take their first real office or those who had outgrown their first office spaces
Technology Involvement	Upped their involvement in the ecosystem, including venture capital and incubators, including joining an appropriate board, so they were meeting weekly with technology entrepreneurs who may have needed help
Marketing Materials	Updated handouts and slide decks that underscored what the team accomplished with copy and imagery that resonated with prospects
Thought Leadership	Helped them author blogs and articles that became part of their marketing tool kit, including one that went viral when they referenced WiredScore, who picked up on it and promoted it

Figure 5-2

Never let a successful project go down in history without documenting it as a case study for future prospects. Include background, the problem, vision and objectives, proposed solution, implementation steps, results, and future applications.

Work hard to exceed your customers' expectations, and never forget to leverage your success by having those happy customers become your best sales reps!

PRO POINTERS

- Happy customers—those for whom you have exceeded expectations—will do more for future sales in your company than your best sales rep.

- The three easiest sales you will ever make:

  1. Repeat sale to a happy customer

  2. Expanded product/service offering to the same customer

  3. Sale to a prospect who's been referred by a happy customer

- Set up the referral/advocacy from the outset: "When we deliver as promised and exceed your expectations, we expect you to do the following on our behalf." Make it contractual if possible.

- Use case studies to continue to differentiate your business and boost your unfair advantage.

- Never hesitate to ask your existing customers for referrals and the opportunity to grow with your client.

- Use recorded and written materials, live mass audience presentations, and one-on-one meetings to leverage your success.

- Never, ever let a success story go down in history without documenting it for future prospecting and marketing.

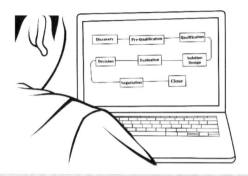

MANAGE THE
SALES PROCESS

Chapter 6

PRIORITIZE PROSPECTS AND SELL EFFECTIVELY

"Most of us spend too much time on what is urgent and not enough time on what is important."

—*Stephen R. Covey*
Business Leader and Bestselling Author

"Sales is a contact sport."

Those are the wise words Ed McLaughlin, founder of USI, once said to me. In order to succeed, according to Ed, you need to have talent, motivation, and a good attitude. You also need to have thick skin and do whatever is ethically required to succeed. These traits proved critical as we grew and knocked open doors.

At USI, we knew we had a unique and disruptive business model, but we were not yet well known. As a result, we didn't get a lot of inbound inquiries, so we had to make the most of the opportunities we generated, which we did by prioritizing our best prospects. Our company mantra was "Prioritize, Focus, and Win."

For any new business or even those attempting to reach the next level of growth, it's easy to fall prey to the shotgun approach—scattering widely to tap every lead that comes onto the radar. You might hit something, but only by good luck will it be the right target for your business.

Instead, it is best to employ the rifle approach, narrowing your focus and targeting the best leads as specifically as possible. Ensure that whatever efforts you employ or the unique content and value proposition you present truly target the right leads and resonate with those prospects. I see too many business owners and their sales reps who are the "jack of all trades, master of none" types. You will never enjoy the Inc. 500–type growth you're aiming for with that approach.

> **A shotgun approach isn't an effective way to target prospects. Use a rifle approach to target your strongest leads.**

To start, you must prioritize your leads, and remember, the lead may not actually be your prospect. The lead may simply be pointing you in the direction of a viable prospect. It may be the data (even as simple as contact information) that identifies a potential buyer, driven by your marketing endeavors. If you fail to prioritize, you'll end up spending equal effort on all leads—the shotgun approach—and you'll ultimately end up wasting valuable time and effort.

Consider this statistic: according to Salesforce, 79 percent of marketing leads never close, and 40 percent of sales reps' time is spent looking for which lead to call.[4] When you do the math, you'll quickly realize that this method is more likely to waste time and effort. Without lead prioritization, energy is spread equally across all opportunities, which makes for lots of unproductive effort.

As a result, it is critical to prioritize leads. Apply the Pareto

---

4 Staff Writer, "6 Ways CRM Helps You Grow Your Business," Salesforce, visited April 13, 2010, https://www.salesforce.com/crm/what-is-crm/how-crm-improves-business/.

principle: 80 percent of your results will come from 20 percent of your effort. It's not about simply generating leads. To really grow your company, you must laser focus on the 20 percent that will bring revenue and offer lifetime value to your company, and you cannot do that unless you prioritize in the first place.

At Midcourse Advisors, to prioritize leads, we use mission-critical components to help our clients as a guide to define and identify ideal clients, develop messaging and marketing, create the offer, and track progress.

Sales Process
Mission-Critical Components

I	DEFINING IDEAL CLIENT	ANSWER
1	Client Criteria and Characteristics	
2	Client Problem(s) to Be Solved	
3	Your Unique Advantage to Solve Problem(s)	
4	Market Size	

II	IDENTIFYING IDEAL CLIENT	ANSWER
1	Tools (LinkedIn, etc.)	
2	Referrals	
3	Partners	
4	Industry Trade Organizations	

III	DEVELOPING YOUR MESSAGING	ANSWER
1	Unique Value Proposition	
2	Accomplishments/Case Studies	
3	Certifications/Recognition	
4	Optimize LinkedIn Profile, Website	

IV	MARKETING YOUR BRAND	ANSWER
1	Events	
2	Publications	
3	Speaking Engagements	
4	Social Media/LinkedIn Activities	

V	CREATING YOUR OFFER	ANSWER
1	Discovery Offer	
2	Other Options for Full Project Engagement	
3	Define ROI for Clients	
4	Get Feedback on Offers	

VI	TRACKING PROGRESS	ANSWER
1	Sales Process Stages	
2	CRM System Implementation	
3	Define ROI for Clients	
4	Get Feedback on Offers	

Figure 6-1

ASSIGNMENT

Time to pause and put what you learned to work.

Fill out your Sales Mission-Critical Components. You can download a template at www.midcourseadvisors.com/growlikeapro.

DRILL DEEPER

Historically, sales reps would qualify and prioritize leads based on the BANT approach: budget (can the prospect afford the solution?), authority (is the prospect the decision maker?), need (is the solution the right fit?) and timing (is the prospect ready to buy now or in the near future?).

While BANT provides a sound starting point, you will still have to drill deeper.

First, I suggest using a prospect Go/No Go tool. Those who score low shouldn't be pursued. Those who qualify should be pursued with rigor. Figure 6-2 provides an example of a Go/No Go tool.

Go/No-Go Checklist

Area	How to Qualify
Client	Never heard of 'em (use Credit Worthiness tool, research litigation history)
	One-time client or repeat client, but not one of our favorites
	Repeat client and one of our favorites
Degree of Difficulty of Response (Proposal Complexity)	First we've heard of it, might be "wired," stiff competition, huge effort to respond to RFP
	Similar project experience, already started to discuss and pull together materials
	We've already been recommended for the team, just need to pull together fee proposal
Strategic Objective	Not really something we should be doing
	Something we've done a good bit of, but don't see as a strategic objective
	Something we've done a lot of and we'll continue to excel in
	Will further our strategic goals of long-term growth, profitability, and internal excitement
Staffing / Risk	We'd have no clue, would probably need to hire outside help or subconsultants
	Schedule is so red-hot that we couldn't successfully support
	A reach for us technically, but not something that we couldn't get a handle on
	No-brainer, could do it in our sleep
Likely Profitability	Questionable ability to even break even, including delivery risk (resources/SOW/etc.)
	Shouldn't be an issue
	No-brainer that we can make a killing

Figure 6-2

Range of Points Possible	Company A	Company B
2		
11	11	
20		20
2		
11	11	
20		20
2		
5		
12		
20	20	20
2		
2		
11	11	
20		20
2	2	
11		11
20		
Total	55	91

0–50
Low side -
Run away!

51–79
Review levers
to increase
opportunities.

80–100
High side -
Go get it!

You can set your criteria as you see fit. For a downloadable Go/No Go Tool, go to www.midcourseadvisors.com/growlikeapro.

As you'll recall from Chapter 4, Gain Attention and Traction, to reach the tipping point and cross the chasm toward greater appeal and acceptance, those in the early majority who have a real pain point are your best prospects. You want to focus on those pragmatists who didn't care to be on the bleeding edge, but are now faced with a situation that is going to force them to move, whether or not they really want to.

In any sales situation, the more you can shine a light on a pain point and then show the value of your solution, the closer you are to closing every sale and growing your business. To accomplish this, I recommend employing a process-driven approach called the Sales Stakeholder Matrix, or SSM, to quantify such pain points. When you quantify your prospect's pain points, you can better customize and present your solution, addressing the needs of all stakeholders and getting to "Yes" faster.

The SSM method identifies the four primary stakeholders and the six questions to solve a pain point. The tool or matrix is shown in Figure 6-3:

Sales Stakeholder Matrix

Pain Assessment/ Stakeholders	Economic Buyer	User Buyer	Technical Buyer	Coach
Describe problem				
How do you measure it today?				
Where are you now?				
Where do you want to be?				
What would achieving desired state mean to you?				
What is the gap between current and desired state?				
What is its impact over time?				

Figure 6-3

ASSIGNMENT

Time to pause and put what you learned to work.

Create a Sales Stakeholder Matrix for your top prospects. You can download a template at www.midcourseadvisors.com/growlikeapro.

As you can see, there are several stakeholders you need to get to say yes to win a new piece of business. According to the well-known Miller Heiman strategic sales training process, these include an Economic Buyer, a User Buyer, a Technical Buyer, and a Coach.

You must consider and address each one in today's buying

environment. The days of striking a deal with a single person in any organization are pretty much history, and in well-managed organizations, those with buying authority don't see themselves as monarchs. They're going to ask for input from those who have to execute on the solution.

> **The days of one person making a buying decision are over. You need to address the four types of buyers: Economic, User, Technical, and Coach.**

The Economic Buyer is the one with the financial authority, including the budget and the checkbook. This person can say yes to an opportunity if the cost to implement and the ROI align with his or her desired goals.

The User Buyer is the professional or set of professionals who will be enjoying the benefits of the product or service on a daily or regular basis. As a result, they can say yes to an opportunity if they believe it will help them do their work more efficiently and effectively.

The Technical Buyer is the subject matter expert. This individual is the professional who knows about the product or service proposed based on past training and/or experience. This person can say yes to an opportunity if he or she believes the solution will fill the pain gap and solve the problem.

Finally, the Coach is the professional who believes in the product or solution by virtue of prior experience, personal relationships, and/or other reasons and can therefore help educate and facilitate to help the other stakeholders get to yes.

Addressing these stakeholders through a Sales Stakeholder Matrix helps you identify their pain points, their desired state (better situation/less pain), the gap between the two, and how your solution can bridge that gap. This will give you the tools and thought processes to help ensure you get to yes.

KEY QUESTIONS

Start by discussing with the prospects the current status of their business—that is, their current business processes in relation to your solution. This is how you can arouse their pain by asking about the domino effect that their problem creates as well as its true impact on the bottom line, customer satisfaction, and perhaps employee morale.

For example, employee retention can be a huge pain point that a staffing company may address. Beyond asking for data in terms of turnover percentages, the staffing company sales rep should be following the problem downstream and asking increasingly probing questions:

- What immediate impact occurs with a resignation?
- How does that impact other departments?
- How much time do you spend on recruiting and hiring replacements?
- Who's responsible for that and how does it keep that person from carrying out their other primary duties?
- How much time do you spend training new employees and when do they really become productive?
- How's employee morale overall?
- What's your customer reaction to working with new, less experienced employees?
- Are you losing customers?

Pain points are effectively problems, and they can certainly be as diverse as your prospective customers. However, they typically fall into the same broad categories with some overlap between them:

Pain Points

Category	Description
Financial	Spending too much money on the current provider, solution, or product and want to cut costs
Productivity	Wasting too much time on what they currently do and a desire to increase efficiency
Process	Needing to improve internal processes
Support	Not receiving the support they need or were promised by their current provider, solution, or product

Figure 6-4

The questions to ask the stakeholders quantify their pain and subsequently prove how you can deliver a solution and address their individual value drivers. Questions include:

- How do you measure it today? (e.g. KPIs, etc.)
- Where are you now? What is your current state?
- Where do you want to be?
- What is the gap between current and desired state— the pain?
- What is its impact over time?

In going back to our example of the problem of retention and its impact on employee morale, here's how those questions may play out at the management level:

Question	Answer
How do you measure?	Well, we don't really measure. We kind of go by a gut feeling and sense intuitively that people are unhappy.
In your current state, on a scale of 1–10, how would you rate employee satisfaction?	I'd give it a 5 . . . maybe even a 4 on some days.
Where would you like to be?	10 out of 10!
What would achieving the desired state mean to you?	Much better morale, leading to greater productivity, leading to more success.
What's the gap?	4–5 points. It's pretty substantial.
What's the long-term impact?	Unhappy employees will contribute to retention loss, and that brings a lot of lost productivity and added cost of hiring and training.

Figure 6-5

Getting your prospects to really understand and honestly admit the gap between their current state and where they want to be is key to agitating their pain. With their pain defined and your solution understood as the pain alleviator, you'll take great strides in closing the deal with your prospects.

With the pain clearly identified, it's time to ask your prospect about their envisioned ideal state. "Where would you like to be? What does the best solution look like to you?"

It is critical to quantify the ROI of your solution and prove that quantified value and pain relief make it desirable.

Finally, note that all the questions are open-ended, prohibiting yes/no answers. This enables you to gain more context and a better understanding to be able to collect information and probe further.

FEASIBILITY-BENEFIT MATRIX

Once you have completed the SSM and know what a "win" is for each stakeholder, you should think about ease of implementation or feasibility. We covered a feasibility-benefit matrix in "Gain Attention and Traction," and it applies here as well. If you get a yes, but it is virtually impossible to properly implement, you will likely have cost and time budget overruns and an unhappy customer. For each solution you present that solves a pain point, you should also address feasibility. Those that have the highest impact or ROI with the highest feasibility are likely those to address first.

An example of a high likelihood of implementation success that would be worth emulating is working with a client on a technology installation that had a fully staffed IT department that also had capacity and the desire to implement your solution. On the other hand, if a client didn't have the capital expenditure budget or the will to change, it may not be worth pursuing as fervently.

The Feasibility-Benefit Matrix

Figure 6-6

In service-based businesses, you're selling an intangible, so it is critical to clearly delineate to your prospect the current pain and future gain in order to make your solution more tangible. Plus, the more well-defined the pain you relieve and gain you facilitate is, the greater the level of fee elasticity you can enjoy. Fee elasticity refers to how sensitive customers may be about your price. The more narrowly defined and quantified the solution is, the greater the price elasticity.

PRO POINTERS

- You cannot be all things to all people. Statistics prove that in order to grow, you must target effectively. Focus on your best client opportunities and don't try to sell to others outside that zone.

- Lead prioritization is critical to avoid wasting valuable time and effort.

- The more you can shine a light on a pain point and demonstrate the value of your solution, the closer you are to closing every sale.

- Use the Sales Stakeholder Matrix to ensure you are addressing the concerns of each type of buyer.

- Validate the ROI of your solution and prove that cost savings and pain relief make it affordable.

- Start with your prospect's current state and follow the impact of the problem downstream.

- Pain points can generally be categorized: financial, productivity and process-related, and support.

- There are three classes of stakeholders that you must address: workflow, management, and the overall organization.

- Ask six defined questions at each of the stakeholder levels to address their pain points and prove how your solution will deliver the desired gain.

- Feasibility must be considered and addressed from the start, or the result will be budget overruns and unhappy customers.

Chapter 7

KNOW YOUR COMPETITION

"In a crowded marketplace, fitting in is a
failure. In a busy marketplace, not standing
out is the same as being invisible."

—Seth Godin
Author and Business Executive

In conducting your market research, either on your own or with the help of an experienced business consultant, you have identified your competition. You know who and how many there are. You've also learned whether they're well capitalized. It may seem daunting, but knowledge is power. You must have a clear picture of your competition in order to win.

You may think that having less competition falls in the plus column of your market research. Maybe. Maybe not. Keep in mind that fewer competitors can be a direct indicator of a solution for a problem without a lot of need. Customers are not clamoring for it, so fewer vendors offer it. You have much greater chance for growth and success offering a solution for which there is a great need and competition than the inverse. It's the old "better to be a big fish in a small pond than a small fish in a big pond" type of thinking.

There are tried and true approaches to get ahead and stay ahead of your competition, and let me start by telling you that pricing is generally not one of them. You may initially be very competitive with pricing when launching your business, but it's a very rare enterprise that builds an empire on low prices. Yes, they exist (think Walmart), but when you compete on price alone, you'll find that you are almost always in cutthroat competition, and you develop a customer base that sticks with you only until someone else offers a lower price. Customer loyalty is tied to price rather than value. In this type of business, profit—already very slim due to price reduction—is only sustained by massive volume. If the volume drops, you'll find yourself on a very slippery slope.

> **Never try to compete on price alone!**

In addition to knowing your competition in order to stay ahead, be aware of your prospects and customers and keep your finger on the pulse of what drives them. Continually monitor what they need and want. When these concerns change and you don't change, you'll find your competitors passing you by. Hand in hand with knowing what your prospects and customers want, be certain you are always looking after your existing customers and delivering the highest level of service to them—well beyond what they expect. Otherwise, they can easily become your competitor's next new customers. There is no shortage of research that shows that vendor indifference is a leading reason why customers leave.

Differentiate yourself. You should already have a solid handle on how you differentiate yourself based on your BMC. Recall that before you even came up with your solution, you created your unique value proposition: the single, clear, compelling message that states why you are different and worth buying! The more you differentiate yourself, the greater the distance you create between you and your competitors.

Be the best employer. Growing and thriving companies have the most skilled team members. In order to attract the best team, you must create an environment and culture in which talented employees want to work along with competitive wages and benefits, with the latter being less important than the former.

Step up your marketing to enhance your brand and connection. Your brand is the image/feeling any customer, partner, employee, or other stakeholder gets when they interact with your company, its products, and/or its services.

You must continually tell prospects about your solution and your organization and why they should buy from you, why you're different, and why your product or service is the best solution for them. Hand in hand with marketing is your image. Ensure that it is inviting, professional, and reflective of your unique value proposition and what your organization stands for. Maybe people shouldn't "judge a book by its cover," but almost everyone does.

FIND WHITESPACE

In the words of "Wee Willie" Keeler, one of baseball's earliest inductees to the Hall of Fame: "Keep your eye on the ball and hit 'em where they ain't." It's sound business advice in terms of finding whitespace.

There are probably as many definitions of business whitespace as there are business gurus. Some define it as a place without competition; others see it as an entirely new market. Still others refer to gaps in existing markets or product lines as whitespace. Regardless of definition, it represents opportunity—opportunity that your competition has not yet uncovered or that your competition has overlooked.

> **Be aware of whitespace. This represents opportunity that competitors don't know about or have overlooked.**

The computer mouse is a great example. Many people think the mouse is an Apple product. In fact, the mouse as we know it today was actually invented by Bill English, working for Xerox at its Palo Alto Research Center (PARC). However, it was Steve Jobs who saw the greater application—the whitespace—and ran with it.

Here's another example. Fitness is a huge industry with a huge market. It's also wildly competitive with at least a handful of franchise gyms and independent studios in every single community. Studio 348 (3-4-8 actually spells "fit" on a keypad), a local gym in my community, found whitespace by targeting a specialized customer group—women over forty who are not in the best shape and who do not enjoy working out or going to the gym. Every aspect of this business caters to this market. The founder carved a niche and created her own whitespace and grew a successful enterprise in a very competitive market.

When we covered prioritizing prospects, I suggested you shoot with a rifle rather than a shotgun. Now I'll take that one step further: don't just shoot with a rifle; shoot with a rifle where there is opportunity! Have a clear target where no one else is shooting.

Some companies fail to capture the opportunities that whitespace offers because it may mean changing their business approach or shifting direction from their original core competencies. This may have been the issue at Xerox with the mouse and other computing products they developed at PARC—they saw themselves in the imaging business, not the personal computer business.

REAL-WORLD EXAMPLES

At USI, we saw the need for integrated services, not just brokerage, so we altered our approach and targeted the CFO rather than the real estate director, offering more value by redirecting our efforts. Similarly, at IEM, we found whitespace by being a disrupter between the hauler and real estate owner. We actually uncovered space to better manage the process by reducing cost and adding value—something our competitors were not doing.

To uncover your whitespace, take a hard look up and down your value chain and do so with a new perspective. Your best opportunities may not always be obvious, especially when you look at your business model and organization the same way all the time. Whitespace can be uncovered by asking questions of your existing customers. What do they need that you are not currently offering? Where is there greater value that you can provide to them?

As an example, I worked with a client called Air Methods. This company provides a unique service: emergency medical transportation for people requiring urgent critical care, serving both communities and hospitals. There is a lot of competition in this industry. What separates Air Methods is its ability to respond most quickly to a patient need, as every second counts. So, when a company enters a market, even if it has competition, it demonstrates its ability to serve faster and therefore better.

Many entrepreneurs shy away from this approach, concerned that they are migrating from their original core competency. They don't want to take a risk on the unknown, so they retreat back to their core or at least to very close adjacencies. Again, smart entrepreneurs always keep the opportunity for growth, including new revenue streams, in clear focus.

Using this externally focused perspective—looking for gaps in existing markets or products/services—to uncover areas that are underserved or unserved is one approach. Another way is to look internally at your team members and their skill sets and your processes to determine how efficiently and effectively you can react to new opportunities. Can you create new opportunities by expanding the use of the skill sets within your organization? What unique skills do you currently have at hand that can be leveraged for growth?

Sometimes it is very difficult for an entrepreneur to take the blinders off and see the company and its opportunities or even threats from a different perspective—a perspective that can lead to growth and avoid failure. As with conducting market research, using a business consultant to help with this exercise often brings with it a very solid ROI—in terms of both money and time. In addition to revenue and profit growth, improving the time you take to bring new ideas and services to market is a great way to beat your competition to the punch.

PRO POINTERS

- Finding less competition is not necessarily a positive. It may indicate a lack of need or desire for your solution.

- Trying to succeed and grow your business on a low-price model is difficult because there is no customer loyalty from people who buy on price alone. Focus on value instead.

- Whitespace represents opportunity that your competition hasn't uncovered or has overlooked.

- Capitalizing on whitespace may mean a shift away from your original intention.

- Uncover whitespace by looking both up and down your value chain to see where new opportunities may exist.

Chapter 8

MANAGE YOUR PIPELINE

"You can't manage what you can't measure."

—Peter F. Drucker
Harvard Professor and Management Authority

You simply won't know where you are in the game unless, of course, you are managing your company and the sales process and keeping score of your progress. In any business, there are countless key metrics that you can track; the key to generating growth is to track and focus on those that will have the greatest impact on your bottom line. Sales probably leads that list.

However, unless you take steps every day to manage your pipeline, you ultimately won't have sales to track. You must ensure that you are always pursuing activities that support your goal and move you toward closing more sales.

The most productive sales reps understand that the value they bring to their respective organizations is their ability to create and nurture relationships with prospects and customers. That requires a human element, so that is their focus. They leave the rest to technology and automation to the fullest extent possible.

Time truly is money, and automation can be a huge time saver—when used correctly. Email is the perfect example of that and epitomizes the double-edged sword. It certainly expedites communication but can simultaneously be the biggest time suck in your day. According to *Forbes,* on average, workers receive two hundred email messages every day and spend 2.5 hours reading and replying.[5] Email is a constant interruption to your day unless you manage it correctly.

Keep emails short, to the point, and sent only when necessary. Get in the habit of setting aside blocks of time to read and reply to email rather than doing so every time one arrives. And turn off the email notification indicator. Tim Ferriss, author of *The 4-Hour Workweek* and noted podcaster, suggests that your email inbox is "everyone else's agenda for your time."[6]

Regain control with apps and tools that allow you to optimize your use of email rather than letting it control you. In addition to turning off the notification indicator and scheduling set time for reviewing messages (and don't set that time as first thing in the morning), take advantage of filters and set rules for the dispensation of incoming messages. During your set review time, read messages once and reply. Then move on. Use your signature line to encourage senders to call you. Nothing indicates the need for a phone call more than emails pinging back and forth!

Take time to set up intelligent automation to indicate senders, subject lines, deal sizes, etc. and take advantage of keyboard shortcuts. Automate, automate, automate—from keyboard shortcuts to deal approvals and everything in between. It can and should be done, and using the excuse that you don't have time won't fly. Salesforce Master Solution engineer Iman Maghroori puts it best: "Saying that you're too busy to automate is like furiously digging

5 Annabel Acton, "How to Stop Wasting 2.5 Hours on Email Every Day," *Forbes,* July 13, 2017, https://www.forbes.com/sites/annabelacton/2017/07/13/innovators-challenge-how-to-stop-wasting-time-on-emails/#3551f3a19788.

6 Tim Ferriss, "9 Habits to Stop Now," July 2018, in *The Tim Ferriss Show,* podcast, transcript at https://tim.blog/wp-content/uploads/2018/07/09-tim-ferriss-the-9-habits-to-stop-now.pdf.

holes with your bare hands and saying you're too busy to look up and grab a shovel."[7]

When you are able to secure a sales meeting, your calendar invitation should always be meaningful and demonstrate benefit. For example, if your prospect is ACME Inc., you shouldn't put "ACME Meeting" in the subject line. Instead, state, "Growing ACME Brand and Market Share."

You should use a calendar software program that enables you to set up reminders before the meeting to ensure participants attend and show up on time. In turn, if they do need to cancel or postpone, it's better they tell you in advance than on the day of the meeting. I currently use Calendly, but there are many other low-cost options.

When you conduct a meeting, you should set an agenda. Ideally, you send it in advance, which gives everyone a chance to see what is being addressed and helps reduce anxiety related to adding value to the meeting or other priorities. When I host meetings, instead of listing topics to be discussed, I try to list questions to be answered. For example, instead of a topic titled "Discuss budget opportunities," consider a question such as "How to generate $100K more EBITDA by the end of the quarter?"

> **Make meetings more productive by sending out an agenda ahead of time with a list of questions to be answered.**

When the meeting is over, immediately schedule follow-up actions or the next meeting. This keeps the sales process moving. If there is resistance, this will tell you something about the prospect's prioritization or what issues you may have to overcome.

---

7   Iman Maghroori, "What's Keeping Sales Organizations from Automating?" Salesforce, visited April 13, 2020, https://www.salesforce.com/quotable/articles/keeping-sales-organizations-from-automating/.

CRM SYSTEMS

If you are considering a CRM or aren't certain your current one is effective, ask the following key questions:

- What are our most inefficient systems and what do we want to improve with a CRM system?

- What process and/ or operational workflows are lacking?

- Who is going to use the CRM system and how many users will we have?

- What other software should integrate with it?

- What's the budget?

CRM systems (customer relationship management) are often viewed as tools to track sales performance. Though the reporting function is important, especially for sales managers, the key benefit is to be able to schedule next steps in the pipeline to prompt ongoing activity to move prospects through or out of the pipeline.

There are many CRM systems available, and they are constantly improving. Most will combine your calendar and inbox along with CRM data, so everything interfaces and syncs easily in real time. They allow you to track leads, sales, and post-sales activities as well as allowing you to easily create reports and intuitive dashboards, keeping your key metrics front and center.

You must manage your pipeline effectively to ultimately close sales, increase revenue, and grow. Your entire staff can synchronize every step of customer interaction from marketing and sales to customer service and post-sale support.

With those questions answered, Figure 8-1 highlights factors you should consider.

Evaluating a CRM System

Aspect	Description
Deployment	Cloud vs. on premise; both have pros and cons.
Features	Find the balance between buying features you'll never use and being well positioned for future growth.
Integration	Ensure that the CRM system will integrate with other software you currently use that the CRM will not replace (e.g. ERP or accounting/HR software).
Demo/Free trial	Never accept it at "face value." At the very least, you must get a live demonstration, but ideally, you can start test-driving a trial version to ensure it meets your needs.
Industry specific	Look for a vendor who specializes in your industry, ideally one with local reps.
Customization and training	An out-of-the-box solution will probably not integrate as you want/need it to. Ask about how it can be customized, the cost for doing so and the level of training and support that is offered.
User experience	Ease of CRM use and how intuitive it is are critical factors. Are buttons clearly labeled? Is the flow of actions logical? Make these determinations during the demo/free trial period.
GDPR Compliance	GDPR (general data protection regulation) went into effect in May 2018 and impacts customers' data storage. Customers can ask to be removed from your database or request an electronic report of what you have stored about them. Your CRM systems should be able to provide this action and information with relative ease.

Figure 8-1

Salesforce is one of the leading CRM systems and is designed for larger enterprises. Depending on the size of your company, you may consider a less robust—and less expensive—alternative. Pipedrive is one that I've often recommended to my clients, as it has a shorter learning curve, is easier to use, and is less expensive. Apto is also a solid product for commercial real estate.

PRODUCTIVITY IMPACTS

One of the features to consider in adding or upgrading automation in your business is the dashboard. There is no point in gathering data if you are not going to put it to use, and there is plenty of good data that can help you prioritize what your next steps in the sales process and in your business as a whole should be.

Well-built dashboards should be customized to present sales data and trends in real time from which you can draw sound conclusions and actionable insights. Plus, they should be responsive, so you can view them on your desktop, tablet, or phone.

Reporting capabilities should be in every team member's hands—from the sales rep to the CEO, enabling forecasting, managing the pipeline, tracking behavior and activities, and identifying when needed steps are not happening. Investment in this type of automation and technology always pays off. Consider this statistic reported by Salesforce Research in its second annual "State of Sales" report: "High-performing salespeople are 11.3x more likely than underperformers to rate their team's analytics and insights capabilities as outstanding."[8]

In addition to data analytics, you can improve productivity by getting rid of the small but insidious time wasters. Not sure what they are? Remember that anything that gets measured improves. So, find an app to use to track exactly how you and your team members are spending your time. Start measuring and you may be very surprised by the results. Use this data to eliminate that which doesn't need to get done and automate as much of the rest as possible.

---

8 Salesforce Research, "Secrets of the Most Productive Salespeople," in Second Annual State of Sales, Salesforce, November 2016.

Finally, every night, schedule your highest-priority activities for the following day. Knowing what you have to accomplish during the day enables you to hit the ground running. Again, checking email should never be a "first thing in the morning" activity. No matter what automation you use to keep track of your calendar and to-do list, the key is preplanning, and it is best done at the end of each day.

Control the day or it will control you. When your day controls you, you'll never come out ahead.

PRO POINTERS

- Statistics show that the bulk of any sales rep's activities are not focused on selling. The good news is that most of those activities can be automated.

- Leverage automation from the simplest to even the most complex task.

- Good CRM systems allow you to track leads, sales, and post-sales activity as well as easily create needed reports and intuitive dashboards, keeping your key metrics front and center.

- Everyone in your organization should have easy-to-customize dashboards that present the data they need for decision-making.

- Get rid of the time-wasting tasks that don't need to be done in the first place and automate the rest.

Chapter 9

LEVERAGE SOCIAL MEDIA

"We don't have a choice on whether we do social
media, the question is how well we do it."

—Erik Qualman
Author of Socialnomics

There are numerous ways to employ technology in your business, from keeping score and monitoring metrics to streamlining processes and procedures. One critical area that may be overlooked is the use of social media. Even in the business-to-business or B2B environment, you can leverage social media to grow your business.

One of the steps in the BMC model that we discussed in Chapter 1 was creating and communicating your unfair advantage—that which cannot be easily copied or purchased. No doubt a huge part of your business's unfair advantage is your own expertise. Your knowledge and insights about your product or service and the industry in which you operate, coupled with the right use of social media, puts you on the path to attracting and retaining more customers and increasing your revenue and profitability—a.k.a. growth.

Today's buyers focus on value, much more so than price. A substantial component of the value you deliver is your knowledge and experience and that of your team or the benefit your product provides. Social media is a great vehicle for imparting that wisdom via the content you post. Consistently create value with your social media posts and you will continue to grow your following.

In addition, Gartner, a global research and advisory firm, reports 85 percent of customers' interactions with brands now take place without speaking to a human.[9] In the past, customers would speak to a sales rep when they wanted to learn about a product or service. Now, they can conduct their own research and will contact you when they're ready to engage, so providing content that educates and answers questions through every stage of the sales cycle is imperative. Case studies that demonstrate how you solved a customer problem as well as reviews and testimonials are effective because potential customers believe in what experiences and beliefs their peers have about you, not what you say about yourself.

We are all inundated with information today, and much of that comes in the form of advertising. There are distractions at every turn, quite possibly with social media leading the way. Many business owners complain that social media is a waste and doesn't deliver results. Without the right plan and approach, you may find yourself with that same complaint.

As with any marketing, results will not be immediate. Everyone would like to catch lightning in a bottle with the post that goes viral; however, odds generally do not favor that. You will only gain a return on your social media investment with consistency. Use social media to create and communicate your thought leadership and also stay top of mind with your customers and prospects with a plan and calendar built around that plan. Without that, social media is likely to be a huge waste of time and money, and you will be hard pressed to measure any results it may deliver.

---

9   Heather Pemberton Levy, "Gartner Predicts a Virtual World of Exponential Change," Smarter with Gartner, October 18, 2016, https://www.gartner.com/smarterwithgartner/gartner-predicts-a-virtual-world-of-exponential-change/.

> ## Social media can be useful if it is consistent, but results will not be instantaneous.

Blogging and article writing should also be part of your marketing tool kit. Share useful and relevant information regularly on a drip basis. No one responds to an information dump because no one has time to read it. Delivering content in digestible chunks increases the likelihood of prospects reading your blogs and articles and serves as an ongoing reminder of your company and your expertise.

Additionally, start to build a library of podcasts and videos. Not all of your customers and prospects want to receive information in the same way. Some want to read; some want to listen; some want to watch. Regardless, whatever you have to say must be relevant and valuable. The value of the content you deliver is directly proportional to the number of followers you gain. You cannot use social media platforms simply as advertising vehicles. Always say something useful and valuable.

Attention-gaining content does not have to be difficult to create, nor does it have to be lengthy. In fact, shorter often wins the day, since most people are pressed for time and already inundated with other things vying for their time and attention. Recall the earlier example I shared about Elfin Realty and its on-the-fly videos in which the employees shared extremely relevant content daily.

Keep in mind that there are various stakeholders at different levels when determining the topics to cover. Alter your topic and approach to address each of the three different types to stakeholders: senior management, middle management, and workflow level. Determine which social platforms your prospects and customers use and focus most of your efforts there. Don't assume; research and ask questions. Ensure your profile and your company's profile are polished and keep them updated. Position yourself as the expert you are.

In developing your messaging and content, stay focused on your unique value proposition and your accomplishments. Using case studies provides a wealth of content about your success. As we did at USI, with the permission of your customers, share their stories in a way that promotes you both. Never hesitate to announce every certification and recognition that you receive. Ditto for your key team members.

Tie all this in to your LinkedIn and other social media profiles and include it on your website. Doing so increases the visibility of both and continues to add to your unfair advantage.

PLAN AND CALENDAR

I could write an entire book on how to create Facebook ads and use lead magnets on social media to create an effective sales funnel. There are numerous resources to help instruct you in this area (e.g. books, online, service providers).

As these methodologies change frequently, I chose to stick to the fundamentals of adding value to your audience and being consistent in your approach.

One way to remain consistent is to use a simple spreadsheet like the one below to create your social media plan for the year and across all platforms:

Social Media Calendar

Date	Topic	Copy	Facebook	Twitter	LinkedIn	Link or Image	Notes
Wk. 1	New Year's	Happy New Year!	Poll: Did you set annual goals?	GIF or fireworks	What is your company's strategy for the year?	Fireworks or soccer goal	Post had record # of likes and shares on FB
Wk. 2							
Wk. 3							
Wk. 4							

Figure 9-1

PRO POINTERS

- Today's buyers focus on value rather than price. A significant degree of the value you deliver is your own expertise.

- You will only gain a return on your social media investment with consistency. The drip approach works best.

- Use social media to create and communicate your thought leadership and remain top of mind with your customers and prospects.

- Deliver valuable content in digestible chunks in various formats—blogs, podcasts, videos, etc.

- Plan out a month's or even a year's worth of content to facilitate and prioritize social media posting.

Chapter 10

IMPLEMENT PRODUCTIVITY HACKS

"Focus on being productive instead of busy."

—*Tim Ferriss*
Author of The 4-Hour Workweek

Your competition is always trying to win business that you want or take away business you already have. To combat this, it pays to be productive. There are several key strategies you should incorporate into your daily practice.

First, you need to win the morning. To do so, get prepared the night before; eat right, exercise, and get plenty of rest so you're both physically and mentally prepared for the day. The highest achievers plan their days the night before so they can digest what they are expecting to encounter and can visualize it, so they hit the ground running.

Once at your desk, block out your day and limit interruptions where possible. Too often, we get interrupted by emails, texts, calls, and coworkers coming to talk to us. Don't let the email monster get you. Make sure to focus on the task at hand, like knocking out ten sales calls.

Use technology to help you be most productive on the go. According to Salesforce, 72 percent of high-performing salespeople optimize use of the sales activities on their smartphones.[10] Configure your phone so you can manage email, dictate messages with voice-to-text, use your CRM, schedule meetings, and make calls.

Delegate or eliminate low-impact tasks. Is browsing through LinkedIn or researching companies taking an inordinate amount of time? If so, delegate it. When I work with clients, we spend two weeks tracking how they spend their time. It's amazing when you look back and see how much time is spent on unimportant administrative tasks that don't need to be done at all, can be done later, or can be delegated.

Be productive with your productive time. When you have calls, be prepared. Do your homework in advance so your calls will have the greatest impact. Check your email at preset times only. Create agendas for meetings when you need to collaborate and stick to the agenda, always ending the meeting on time.

Do your work at the best times for you. Some people are morning people (myself included). Others are night owls. Spend your best and most focused energy addressing the hardest challenges when you are freshest and mentally prepared.

Similarly, make sure to reach out to the people you seek to contact at the best times to reach *them*. If you are trying to contact business executives and don't have a scheduled call, the ideal times are often early in the morning or late in the afternoon, when they may be at their desks rather than in meetings. If you are trying to avoid their administrative staff (a.k.a. "the Gatekeepers"), dialing or emailing at those times is often more effective as well.

---

10 Prina Mandavia, "5 Tips to Maximize Your Sales Team's Productivity," Salesforce, March 14, 2017, https://www.salesforce.com/uk/blog/2017/03/5-tips-to-maximise-your-sales-teams-productivity.html.

PRO POINTERS

- Win the morning or waste the rest of your day.

- Limit interruptions and use technology to the greatest extent possible.

- Many tasks can be delegated, done later, or not done at all.

- Be prepared for meetings, stick to the agenda, and never adjourn without setting action steps.

- Do your most important work at the time of day when you are sharpest.

TOGETHER
EVERYONE
ACHIEVES
MORE

LEAD THE RIGHT TEAM

Chapter 11

HIRE WELL

"Hiring the right people takes time, the right
questions, and a healthy dose of curiosity."

—Richard Branson
Founder of Virgin Group

Your team—the human capital of your company—is the foundation for generating and sustaining growth. Having the right team starts with making the right hires.

Of course, you want team members who will always give 100 percent; however, you don't want the math to work out like this:

12%	Monday
23%	Tuesday
40%	Wednesday
20%	Thursday
5%	Friday
100%	

Focus on hiring smartly in the first place and treat people well after they're hired, and you'll avoid this type of "100 percent" mentality.

Let's take a minute to revisit Newton's Laws of Motion. His first law was that an object at rest will remain at rest unless a force acts upon it. At the same time, an object in motion will not change its acceleration unless a force acts upon it. Newton wasn't focusing on success and performance at the office, but his theories actually can apply there. To put the first law of motion into more current terms: "Showing up is half the battle." You have to act to overcome inertia.

To build on the concept of overcoming inertia, think about going to the gym. Even for those who enjoy working out, actually getting to the gym is half the battle. It's true for me. I struggle to get up early on dark, cold mornings to head to the gym, but once there, I'm raring to go and enjoy the workout.

Like "showing up," hiring well is really half the battle to creating a team that enjoys serving clients and enables company growth and success. Attract and engage the team members by showing positive disposition and attitudes and you'll take a huge step forward. The right team members help you develop the right culture—one that will continue to attract the best talent. That's why hiring well is critical.

Much has been said about generational differences in the workforce. It's important to note that millennials will comprise 40 percent of the workforce by 2025. Consider the three concerns that are the focus of millennials' approach to work when you're hiring and aim for the intersecting sweet spot. Note this isn't about job security, promotion opportunity, or monetary considerations.

Figure 11-1

A PLAYERS VS. A−/B+ PLAYERS

Many executives and consultants suggest you always hire *A Players*. This is because proven team members typically provide the best results.

I tend to agree with this philosophy for a new venture or offering because there are only a few team members and the risk is too high.

However, I have found that *A Players* are often the most demanding and hard to mold or coach. As a result, they leave and move to the next opportunity more frequently to further validate themselves via title or compensation or even both.

Consequently, I tend to focus on *A−/B+ Players* because they comprise a larger pool of candidates, cost less, and have more upside.

As shown in Figure 11-2, target the 20 percent that fall just below the *A Player* threshold. I promise you won't regret it, especially in a tight job market.

Hiring Targets

Figure 11-2

WRITE EFFECTIVE JOB DESCRIPTIONS

It's pretty simple. If you clearly communicate what you want and stand out by appealing to qualified candidates, you'll end up with better team members.

Online job posts often seem come from the exact same template with detailed lists of requirements and responsibilities. Yes, you want ten years of industry-specific and five years of functionally specific experience. Yes, you want an advanced degree. Yes, your company is the best thing since sliced bread with all of your years in business, sustainability initiatives, and community service. Every job description starts to sound the same.

If you break from this mold, you'll attract better candidates in the first place. Of course, you have to identify key responsibilities and expectations, but go one step further. Enhance your listing so it more creatively indicates what the job entails. Describe what is different and advantageous about this opportunity and why the job will have an impact and why that impact will matter to the candidate.

Change the perspective and consider what you can do for the candidate rather than solely focusing on what the candidate can do for you. In a *Wall Street Journal* study, researchers determined that more successful postings included statements like, "We seek to provide employees with constructive feedback to foster their career growth," and "You will have the opportunity to collaborate with talented people." Place more focus on what your company will provide to the candidates, and you'll start to attract a better talent pool. Without a talented pool from which to choose, you will always struggle to hire well.

Consider this example of a well-written job description. If I met the qualifications, I would apply in a heartbeat because the culture is obviously fun, the technology is leading edge, and the company is authentic.

Software Engineer

Our passion is building fantastic (and award-winning) products people love. First things first. Working for us will provide you with an amazing work environment.

Amazing how?

- *Work with a proven and incredibly talented team*
- *Work on a new MacBook Pro Retina Laptop and 27" Apple Cinema Display*
- *Open, fun, and comfortable workspace (no cubes!)*
- *We have an in-office barista and coffee bar that keeps us going with beverages and healthy snacks*
- *75" television in work area for work demos and maybe for watching football too*
- *Break-out rooms for small meetings, privacy, quiet space*
- *We have a robot and he pushes code, makes jokes, and runs our automated tests!*
- *Ping-Pong table, Cornhole boards, and Nintendo 64 (bring your A game!)*
- *Be the DJ with Sonos & Jambox speakers throughout the office*
- *Pennant of your university hung with pride in the office*

We're quickly growing both our business and our team and need to fill multiple roles (Junior, Mid, and Senior) on our roster with developers that are passionate about programming and building an amazing product. We need your help both scaling our existing systems and building it to enable our vision: fun, flexible, and memorable!

DRAFT SOUND EMPLOYMENT AGREEMENTS

Having sound agreements is how you should start a relationship with an employee.

There are two critical agreements: the partnership agreement and the employment agreement. The following is not meant to be a primer on how to construct these agreements. Instead, it is an alert to you that having them is essential. Do not start a business without partnership agreements and don't hire additional team members without employee agreements.

> Partnership agreements are not simple documents that can be completed with a handshake or on the back of a napkin. Make sure to get legal representation to ensure that the agreements comply with state and national regulations and the agreement serves your best interests as well as those of the company.

I have seen far too many partners who joined forces to change the world, but then ended up in court because they didn't expect any disagreements and wanted to focus on the business. Likewise, I have seen employees become disgruntled and sometimes quit when they didn't receive the incentive compensation they expected, whether because of a conversation or a misunderstanding of the incentive plan. The following are the key elements that should be covered in any partnership agreement:

Partnership Agreement

Category	Description
Percentage of Ownership	How much each founder/partner/owner retains. This could be based on who had the business idea, who validated the idea, who contributed funds to launch the business, who has the skills and relationships to grow the business, etc.
Allocation of Profits and Losses	How financial success/challenges are attributed. How profits are split or reinvested in the business. How losses are absorbed and how additional funding will be secured.
Decision-Making	Who gets to make major decisions for the company and how is that achieved?
Contractual Responsibility	Based on making decisions, who makes agreements with others (vendors/partners/customers/etc.) and who is responsible for signing checks?

Death of a Partner	It is essential to spell out what happens if a partner becomes disabled or dies.
Dispute Resolution	When a major disagreement occurs, how will it be resolved? And if it can't be resolved and the partnership needs to be changed or dissolved, how is this accomplished?

Figure 11-3

Similarly, when you hire a new team member, the employee agreement you provide to the prospective employee says a lot about your company and its approach to human resources. Key elements of such an agreement include:

Employee Agreement

Element	Description
Welcome	Not typically included, but this section can create a good feeling for the prospective employee while continuing to promote a company's brand. It can include the company's vision and that the prospective employee is expected to help achieve this vision.
Role/Job Description	Indicates in detail what is expected of the individual and also how the employee's contributions will help the company achieve its goals.
Reporting Relationships	The key here isn't just indicating the formal hierarchy, but how the manager is expected to support the employee and help him or her succeed.
Compensation	Base compensation and variable compensation, including commissions and bonuses, should be clearly identified.

Figure 11-4

At USI, just in front of the signature block, every employee agreement contained a statement about the company and its relationship with its team members. It stated:

This employment offer is based on your commitment to USI's standard Business Practices and Operating Philosophy, including:

- *Making commitments and keeping them*
- *Providing total quality in everything you do*
- *Being a team player*
- *Holding yourself accountable to the USI team*
- *Holding the USI team accountable to you*

To me, the last two points were especially meaningful. For the company to succeed, everyone needed to be accountable. At USI, we had a low level of attrition, in large part due to our transparency and clarity at the outset. Those who embraced it joined and stayed; those who didn't never came on board and probably would have left sooner anyhow.

There are many other important elements not as differentiated as those I've just covered including:

- Benefits
- Privacy policies
- Terms of relationship
- Termination guidelines

Similarly, if you have contractors on your team due to variable needs or specific expertise, the contractor agreement can have many, if not all, of the same elements.

Again, get legal representation to ensure this is document is done properly and in your prospective employee's best interests as well as those of the company.

EMBRACE TECHNOLOGY

To connect with and reach your desired audience, in addition to hiring well, you must show that your company is technology-oriented and forward thinking. It's what prospective team members want before they'll even consider working for a company. Studies from MIT and Deloitte found that the large majority of people want to work for such companies, forcing them to invest in this area. Growth and technology investments will forever be linked—in hiring as well as in operations.

If you are interested in specifically attracting millennials, you must have an up-to-date website that is mobile responsive so these candidates can browse on their smartphones.

Additionally, you want to demonstrate that technology is an integral part of your company's DNA and vision. A good example is the recent advertising push by General Electric focusing on its role as a technology company, not just an industrial one, as they migrate toward big data analytics. The result was GE's ability to attract better candidates to its evolving business model.[11]

You can use technology to hire well. Artificial intelligence (AI) applications are being introduced to screen candidates. Although computers can identify patterns for people who will fit the job description and are worth interviewing, there is no substitute for human interaction.

CULTURAL FIT

It's not only critical to attract the best candidates in terms of talent and experience, you have to attract the ones who will be the right cultural fit to your organization. Look around—is your workplace very structured with a business-suit dress code with assigned desks and hours from 8:00 to 5:00? That may be fine for law firms and financial services businesses, but if you want to attract innovative and tech-focused talent, there will almost always be a cultural mismatch. If you're a tech start-up, you'll have to collaborate with a banker, but you may not want to hire one.

It is also important to align personality types within your

11 Jeff Fromm, "What Brands Can Learn from GE about Winning with Millennial Employees," *Forbes,* March 20, 2017, https://www.forbes.com/sites/jefffromm/2017/03/20/what-brands-can-learn-from-ge-about-winning-with-millennial-employees/#2553d7eb2831.

culture. Certain traits are inherent to certain positions. Empathy is far more important to a nurse or social worker than to a programmer or tax attorney. That said, no matter what function your company serves, in order to have a cohesive and effective team, you actually need various personality types. We'll delve into this more fully in Chapter 14, Organize Thoughtfully.

INTERVIEWING SKILLS

Comedian Steven Wright did a bit about the job interview process:

"I was interviewing for a job and the hiring manager was asking me some basic, typical questions. Getting a little bored and antsy with the line of questioning, I opened a book and started reading. Then I said to the guy, 'Let me ask you a question. If you are in a spaceship that is traveling at the speed of light, and you turn on the headlights, does anything happen?' He said, 'I don't know.' I said, 'I don't want your job.'"

It's one of my favorites, and yes, a bit quirky, but it drives home the point that most hiring managers (or those tasked with the responsibility) are not properly prepared to conduct a good interview. If you've attracted the ideal candidates by crafting the perfect job description, demonstrating your tech savviness, and ensuring those candidates are a good cultural fit, it won't matter if you blow it during the interview process. It's more than checking the box about experience and skills. You have to be able to evaluate the soft skills as well. These skills include critical thinking, communication, collaboration, and creativity. I focus on these qualities when I'm interviewing.

Most people focus on the what, as in what gets done. You also have to concentrate on the how, or how things get done when you're interviewing.

The best way to identify soft skills, drive, and ambition is to ask open-ended questions:

- Why did you enjoy your last job?
- How would a boss or coworkers describe you?

- What motivates you to get up early in the morning with great energy, and why?
- Where do you see yourself in three, five, or ten years?
- When did you first fail and how did you handle the failure?

Many people view the hiring process as one of weeding out rather than discovering the best fit, working from a negative rather than positive perspective. I was once asked the following during an interview: "My boss and I have a difference of opinion. He believes that attitude and the ability to learn and grow are the best attributes for a new hire. I believe someone who is loyal who already has all the requisite skills is the best attribute. Who do you think is right, my boss or me?"

That was clearly a loaded question. The hiring manager wanted to see if I was astute enough to provide the right answer as opposed to automatically aligning with him and his stated philosophy. I took a minute or two to think through this question, as it did challenge me. I responded that, although I value loyalty and skills, I preferred hiring people with the right attitude and potential to grow. I shared my previous experience at a company where we attracted and hired a great team based on people we discerned could work hard, be good team members, and be willing to learn and adapt to our business model. We were focused on the long term rather than the transactions, so this required a good filter.

I will caution you against trying to qualify candidates by attempting to trick them. I wasn't offered that position, but I doubt I would have accepted it anyway. The interviewer's approach did nothing to foster trust, and as I said, hiring well means showing candidates what you can do for them as much as what they'll do for you.

HIRE THE BEST AVAILABLE ATHLETE

Sometimes, in the course of managing your business, you may come across a person who doesn't fit a current job description or opening. However, everything else about this individual suggests the individual will be a star at your company. In other words, he or she has a rare combination of expertise, skill, attitude, and ability.

In my experience, when you can find lightning in a bottle, if you can make it work financially, you should hire that person and find a role for him or her.

While leading IEM, I found out Craig Melton was interested in working there. He had worked for me previously at USI and had a very strong operations background. At IEM, we had operational leadership, but I knew Craig could elevate this function, so I hired him as COO. We grew our top line 30 percent in one year after bringing Craig on board, in large part due his efforts to deliver the work more efficiently and effectively.

Athletes understand how to work as part of a team, and that's why they are good hires, especially if you're assembling a winning team for a growing company.

THE ASSIGNMENT APPROACH

One of the methods I've used successfully to hire well is the assignment approach. I give the short-listed candidates a homework assignment to bring to the second interview. I quickly discovered the quality and timeliness of their work as well as their presentation skills and overall confidence to communicate well under pressure. I have found this more helpful than a writing sample or even a reference. The assignment had specific parameters along with the need for some research and preparation of a report.

One time, I was asked to interview candidates and hire someone to lead USI's new Toronto office. Let me share how it played out.

The first candidate was prepared and presented his one-page summary, which was nicely done but did not exceed expectations. Candidate number two was completely unprepared. He had a point of view, but did not provide the requested report. Upon further questioning, it was obvious he thought he could wing the assignment. You can't wing leadership. The last candidate was Goldilocks—everything was "just right." She was in professional attire, wrote a polished report, and expressed gratitude for me pushing her. She saw the assignment as her ability to uncover more about how the company would challenge her and help her grow professionally. Her name was Judy Fancy. She got the job and became a productive and well-regarded team member for many years.

THE 5 Hs

Interviewing new candidates or meeting new people can often be awkward, to say the least. How can you get to know someone quickly and have a genuine and meaningful conversation? How does asking someone their strengths and weaknesses work for anyone? I struggled with this for many years. Often, I feel as if I got lucky meeting quality people, as I have a knack for recognizing people who have great passion and attitude. Because the quality of a service business is so driven by the quality of its people, why leave it to chance?

Fortunately, many years ago, I had the opportunity to meet Matthew Driscoll, the men's basketball coach at the University of North Florida in Jacksonville, Florida. He created a simple methodology, called the 5 Hs, to determine the best fit of potential recruits. His team represents a brotherhood, and was and is far more than just being teammates. He created a culture that has been successful, so he wanted new players to fit.

The 5 Hs

Category	Description
History	Tell me about your background and how it shaped who you are today.
Highlight	Share a success or defining moment and what made it special.
Heartache	Share a challenge, what you did to overcome it, and how it impacted you.
Hero	Tell me who inspires you and why.
Hope	Share what you hope to accomplish as a player, student, and in life.

Figure 11-5

ASSIGNMENT	Time to pause and put what you learned to work.
	List your 5 Hs. Take your direct reports out for a drink and ask them to share the same.

I have and still use this approach often. In fact, I recently interviewed several people for an administrative role, and they all were thrilled with the 5H questions, as it showed I cared about them and their situations, not just their résumé accomplishments.

I also use it in my classes teaching entrepreneurship at Georgia State University. The students enjoy it and have said it allowed them to get to know their classmates far better. In turn, I get to know the students better sooner. Using this methodology, I learned one candidate lost her mother when she was five years old. As a result, she learned to become independent, industrious, and gritty, valuable attributes for an employee.

The 5H approach also serves as an icebreaker, and you may find in implementing this approach that you can conduct the entire interview based on the candidate's answers as the dialog between you unfolds.

FINAL THOUGHTS

Whatever size organization you have, invest in a background check. I've entertained candidates whom I thought would be great team members and actually made offers subject to a background check. The background check will reveal prior lawsuits, bankruptcies, and other red flags. While everyone deserves a second chance, it is critical that you know a candidate's full background before bringing the person onto the team. The red flags may not be deal breakers, but you should never be blindsided by information you should have uncovered early on.

Let me reiterate: interviewing is a two-way street. When you apply all of these techniques to qualified candidates, they are interviewing you at the same time. Personally, I try to put myself in the shoes of the candidates to understand what they are looking for, and if they are qualified and a good fit, they will feel comfortable saying yes to the offer.

PRO POINTERS

- To have a productive, innovative team that will help you expand, you must hire well in the first place.

- You simply cannot hire well if you don't have a solid talent pool from which to choose in the first place.

- Excluding new ventures or offerings, focus on hiring *A–/B+ Players* to grow your business.

- The job description should offer the benefits of working for you and what sets your organization apart as well as the position's requirements and responsibilities.

- Demonstrate that technology is part of your company's DNA.

- Cultural fit is as important as experience, education, and skill.

- Focus on soft skills: critical thinking, communication, collaboration, and creativity.

- Hone your interviewing skills.

- Employ various approaches to discovering the best candidate.

- Conduct a background check so you have the full picture.

Chapter 12

FORM A CULT, CARVE A PATH

"If you want to go fast, go alone. If
you want to go far, go together."

—African proverb

Hiring well is only the first step. Once you've hired, you need to draw others to follow you and embrace your vision in order to achieve and sustain growth. You need to create the right culture in your organization. To do so, you need to create a cult following—a group that is highly passionate and highly dedicated and that fervently worships what they believe in. Yes, it happens with film, musical artists, television series, and video games . . . but it can also happen in business.

Companies like Apple, Yeti Coolers, Trader Joe's, Southwest Airlines, Tesla, and Chick-fil-a have cult followings. These companies' fan bases patronize them repeatedly not just because they like the products and services, but because customers feel a distinct connection with the company's culture, mission, and the way in which they do business.

There are people like Bruce Springsteen and Warren Buffett

who have also generated cult followings. If you've ever been to a Springsteen concert, you know it is four hours of energy and the singer shows a strong connection to the average working person. Poll Springsteen fans and they will tell you that they've followed him for years, attending many concerts in many different venues, often traveling great distances to do so.

It's never been easy to get a Springsteen concert ticket, but it's far easier to see him in person than to attend a Berkshire Hathaway Annual Meeting, led by Warren Buffett. Known as the "Oracle of Omaha," Buffett has developed a cult following for his business investment leadership and financial success. Buffett is relatable; despite being a billionaire, he has lived in the same modest house and has a down-to-earth communication style that's easily absorbed and understood.

These are two very different people serving very different audiences who both have created incredible cult followings.

Finally, companies also have employees who are cult-like. They believe in the company, its leadership, its products/services, and its culture. They feel a part of something bigger than themselves and will therefore go the extra mile, work well in teams, and represent the company extremely well internally, with customers, and in the community.

CREATE A STRATEGIC PURPOSE

If you are passionate about what you do and are an inspiring leader, people will be attracted to you and will follow you. They'll want to learn from you, seeking you out and engaging with you. As an entrepreneur or senior manager, you are no doubt passionate about what you do. In order to build a cult following, you must be able to communicate your passion and the reasons for it.

First, define your organization's Statement of Strategic Purpose (SSP) in order to build and communicate your culture. This can be done for the overall company, a division, a department, or even a small group or team. Documenting the SSP creates meaning for your team's mission and answers and incorporates the following:

Statement of Strategic Purpose

Element	Description
Why We Exist	Describes what you do, why you do it, and what problem you are addressing
How We Operate	Describes how this is achieved/how the problem is best solved
Who We Are	Describes your qualifications to best address the problem to be solved

Figure 12-1

To better understand the importance and impact of the SSP, I'm including one I wrote that I proudly displayed and utilize at Midcourse Advisors each and every day:

Statement of Strategic Purpose

We help companies address strategic opportunities and challenges. Through these shared experiences, we develop trusting, long-lasting relationships adding value throughout the process.

We are focused on management consulting for small and midsize companies. We pride ourselves as a true strategic partner for our customers. We seek to understand the vision, mission, goals, objectives, opportunities, and challenges facing a client now and into the foreseeable future. We guide our clients through development and implementation of the strategic plan. We are able to measure our joint success and address any challenges proactively each and every day. We accomplish this using our tools, expertise, resources, and communication skills we have acquired through our experience.

Our team members are intelligent people who share a compassion for clients and an unparalleled commitment to quality. They are curious by nature and engage to be at the forefront of best practices for B2B services companies. We compensate our team members within the top quartile in the industry and structure the systems so that a combination of salary and bonus enables the right behaviors regarding service and customer satisfaction. We are team oriented and place our clients' needs first. Our offices are open, bright, collegial, and welcoming.

We understand the work we do is important, but life is short and there are other reasons we exist. As a result, we support our team members as parents, spouses, members of families, and contributors to their communities and places of worship.

We hand this document to all candidates interested in working for our firm, and we share it with clients and other stakeholders. We attract talented people, and you can do the same. If you already have a Statement of Strategic Purpose, great, but I encourage you to review it to ensure it covers the three questions I posed and that it communicates your level of passion and commitment. If you don't have one, it's time to write one right now . . . and then share it generously.

ASSIGNMENT	Time to pause and put what you learned to work. Craft a Statement of Strategic Purpose for your business. You can download a template at www.midcourseadvisors.com/growlikeapro.

WALK THE WALK

A Statement of Strategic Purpose is important, but unless there are ongoing behaviors that support the words, it's no more valuable than the paper it may be written on. You have to promote, support, and live the virtues that you describe. Every action and every decision you make should be done through the lens of why you exist, how you operate, and who you are . . . always.

For example, if you espouse long-term thinking and developing long-lasting relationships with clients, reiterate that value to quell discussions that may arise about short-term revenue or profit objectives that place the company rather than the client first. If you say you value the team, your actions and policies must clearly support that and communicate it to each of your team members. When you do what you say—walking the walk—you'll be respected for being authentic and consistent. You'll be building a cult.

> To help build a cult, you must show that you value your team. You must do what you say—walking the walk—and be authentic and consistent.

In developing your cult, it's your job to clearly articulate your values. It isn't your job to convince people to adopt them. Those who believe in you will follow you like the Pied Piper. Those who don't won't. That's self-selection and it should work that way. Those who know me well know that I enjoy the climb more than reaching the mountaintop. However, once there, I will stand and exclaim my values and how they connect and align with others. That doesn't mean I try to convince others to adopt my values and what I believe. I just want to engage with and mentor those who do. I've developed my own cult following as a result of these behaviors and this approach.

If you are fair and treat people well, and have some fun along the way, they will follow you.

BUILD TRUST

We survive because we surround ourselves with other people who believe what we believe—and then trust develops. Keep in mind, there's a big difference between trust and reliability. The latter occurs when you do what you say you are going to do. You say you'll deliver by the end of the day and you do. That's being reliable. That's not trust.

Trust and reliability are not necessarily intertwined. For example, we all have the one friend who's always late and always screwing up. We know he's not reliable, but that does not mean he's not trustworthy. In fact, that person may be the friend you trust the most. Trust is born of common values and beliefs. Your friend is notoriously and consistently late, but you believe and value the same things. You have each other's backs.

With trust, we gain confidence to experiment and attempt new things, try new ideas, and explore new concepts. You must develop trust with customers in order to gain traction.

Almost all businesses begin with a clear link between what they do and why they do it. The founders can clearly envision what they want to achieve and can communicate the vision in such a way that it draws others to the organization. There are shared beliefs and values. The initial core group is quite cohesive in going forward because of those shared visions and beliefs. Trust exists. However, once the organization grows—it is successful at *what* it does—new team members are needed, and there can begin to be a disconnect between what they do and why they do it. The what, or executing on delivering the product or service, might still be working perfectly and growing. The problem begins when those tasked with carrying out the what, no matter their skill or level of expertise, may be fuzzy about the why.

According to well-known business author and consultant Simon Sinek, the divergence of the what and the why becomes obvious when the stress level goes up and the passion goes down. The founders may comment that it's "not like it used to be and it doesn't feel the same anymore." These comments and feelings can occur despite growth and great success. Another symptom of divergence occurs when the company starts to worry more about what the competition is doing than what it is doing.

Three great examples of this divergence of what and why are Apple, Starbucks, and Dell. When Steve Jobs, Howard Schultz, and

Michael Dell left their organizations, respectively, each company began to slide, only to bounce back when each leader returned. They embodied the passion of their organizations, so the why, including why every team member came to work every day, was clear. Trust returned along with the sense of purpose and "why."

In organizations where this divergence between the what and the why increases, distrust of management, employees, and even vendors and customers grows as well. Technology works at every turn to increase the volume and speed of information and communication, but it does nothing to build trust. Trust can only be created when empathy exists. And empathy requires human contact.

Use of technology has limited human contact in far too many organizations. For example, customer service used to mean one-on-one interaction between people, on the phone or in person. Now it's a reply to an email or possibly an online chat box. Actual human contact is often very limited or even nonexistent. Ironically, some companies today are advertising that you can actually speak to a real person! It's as if speaking to someone is a luxury, despite the fact that survival depends on human contact—both at the most basic level and in your business.

As growth, size, and scale become the focus, the human side of business is often overlooked. However, without the human side, there is no trust, and without trust there will never be traction and real growth.

COMPENSATE WELL

When hiring, you have to provide a compensation package that competes with the market to attract good candidates. This includes financial compensation, benefits, vacation, etc.

Just as important as the amount of financial compensation is the compensatory structure. The reason? People behave based on how they are paid.

An example near and dear to me is the real estate business in which brokers are paid commissions and therefore are incentivized to increase the value of the real estate transaction to increase their commission. This was contrary to what clients wanted, given their objective was to have suitable space at the least cost. Another example is Boeing, which recently ran into trouble providing a production rather than a quality incentive; it produced a number of Dreamliner 787 airplanes that malfunctioned.

At USI, we turned the compensation model upside down to better serve clients and our own interests. We paid our employees salaries and added bonuses based on profits. As a result, they didn't need to complete a transaction to pay their bills and took a more partner-like view.

As you bring members onto the team, make sure their rewards are structured to provide them the highest benefit when their performance helps the customers and your company.

CARVING A PATH

With your cult following in place and compensation structured appropriately, it's time to carve a path for your team members to reach the next opportunity. That opportunity may be within your organization or it may be someplace else.

Wait, you're thinking. *I should go to all this work to hire well to build a team and get people to follow me just so I can lead them out the door?*

Not exactly. But you must have a path for growth and the next opportunity. People always want to know what their next step is and what it takes to get there. When your team achieves success and secures the next level of opportunity, that growth is satisfying and helps them flourish. Challenge your staff and provide them with the tools and training they need to meet the challenge. This keeps your team vibrant and motivated. Either you can provide them greater opportunities within your organization or they will find them elsewhere. People want to grow. It's as simple as that.

You can create growth opportunities by creating and implementing programs that challenge your team members, allowing them to learn new skills and enjoy new experiences. These programs can be rotational or transformational. A rotational program gives a team member the opportunity to fulfill a different role for a set period of time in a new department or new business unit. With this exposure, the person gets a broader perspective regarding various aspects of how the organization operates. He can return to his original position with the ability to look at things with a fresh set of eyes, and improvements and innovation often follow quickly.

A transformational program gives a team member the opportunity to fill a role on a specific project or initiative until it is complete. Perhaps it's taking on a leadership role for a small team to implement a new system or to solve a specific challenge. As with a rotational approach, it will test the employee's ability to adapt and add value, often improving and expanding his skill set. Upon completion, the team members may be ready to move up, and you've given them the path to do so.

Companies that take this approach groom their team members for bigger and better jobs, often within the organization. Their growth causes the company to grow. Their loyalty grows with their satisfaction, and loyalty spurs productivity and innovation. Productivity and innovation are the cornerstones for organizational growth!

Work with your team members to understand what they want to achieve and support their journeys. Based on aptitude and desire, some will want to push themselves to fulfill a greater potential they see for themselves. Others may be satisfied with what they are doing and like the routine and stability. That's not necessarily a bad thing. Of course, you can't experience organizational growth with a team that is content to grow very, very slowly, embracing the status quo. However, on the other hand, no company succeeds if the entire team is eying the corner office with the goal of becoming the CEO. You must have the appropriate mix of different types of employees.

For those who have both the potential and desire, take time and make the effort to help them identify the path to their next opportunity with these questions:

- What is the desired opportunity?
- Does the desired opportunity fit the potential? Or is there a better opportunity than what you (the team member) may be currently envisioning?
- What skills do you need to fortify and what experiences do you need to fill any gaps that exist from where you are now to where you want to be?
- What is the desired financial opportunity for both the company and you?

While this is a solid foundation for an annual review, I encourage you not to wait for a once-a-year conversation, because plans change and opportunities may come and go. Your team members think about their job satisfaction every day, not just when their review is approaching. You should also consider how you can help your team to grow with that same regularity. Once a year won't cut it.

If it turns out that an employee's path for growth leads him out your door and on to someplace else, so be it. It is always better to continue to spur the growth of everyone on your team, because by doing so, job satisfaction soars and the environment will be one in which everyone thrives. Proactively discuss your team members' next challenges, opportunities, and rewards and carve out the path for them to achieve those, and you will inspire higher performance and loyalty. You will inspire growth.

PRO POINTERS

- Cult followings exist because people want to associate with something or someone in whom they can believe. Cult followings can occur in business and with your team members.

- Create your Statement of Strategic Purpose by defining:
    - Why you exist
    - How you operate
    - Who you are

- Walk the walk and do what you say in order to get people to follow you.

- Compensating well extends beyond the monetary package. Be certain you structure correctly to avoid undermining service to clients.

- Continually provide opportunities for growth for your employees, or they will find them somewhere else.

- Implement programs that require your employees to learn new skills and broaden their perspectives.

- Don't wait for the annual review to discuss new opportunities.

- Team member growth leads to company growth.

Chapter 13

SET CLEAR EXPECTATIONS

"Connect the dots between individual roles
and the goals of the organization. When
people see that connection, they get a lot of
energy out of work. They feel the importance,
dignity, and meaning in their job."

— Ken Blanchard
Business Leadership Expert
and Author of The One Minute Manager

As we've just discussed, you grow your company by growing your employees. However, you want them to grow according to your plan and vision for your company. The last thing you must do is set clear expectations and communicate them clearly to maintain that alignment.

Typically, in a company's annual planning process, senior leaders evaluate the company's overall direction and where investments, resources, and expertise are needed. They usually push down goals onto their reports, who then do the same for theirs. When this occurs, those team members tasked with the execution often feel they don't understand where the company is headed, what their contributions and impact can be, and how they will be rewarded. As a result, they don't buy in.

A more effective way is to set an overall goal and empower your teams to determine how best to achieve the goal. The team members are typically closer to the customer and therefore better prepared to generate actionable ideas to both grow revenue and manage cost. Once completed, each function or department then has its requisite budget that collectively adds up to meet the overall financial and operational goals.

> **For employees to understand their contributions on impact on the company, encourage them to devise ideas to meet the department and company goals.**

For example, at Deutsche Bank, we worked hard to set clear expectations and also be very transparent about the overall business and departmental goals. There was a clear picture about how each department fit together to bring about the vision. The budget was a sizable figure at one billion euros annually, and each region had its targets based on where the business was headed. The methodology followed the Business Goals in Figure 12.1.

Business Goals

Category	Description
Alignment	We were all rowing in the same direction, and each group was able to see its contribution and what that meant to the whole of the department and ultimately to the company. If the components of my team didn't achieve their plans, then I didn't achieve mine. If my peers and I didn't achieve our collective plans, my manager didn't make his either.
Measurement	We could transparently track and report progress against goals, so everyone knew exactly where we stood at any given time. That enabled teams and individuals to adjust as needed, providing greater opportunity to achieve the plan.
Reward	The reward for accomplishing the plan was simple and clearly communicated and understood. The penalty of lack of reward was equally as simple and clearly understood.

Figure 13-1

As part of the planning, each individual set clear goals for the year according to the SMART goal methodology: Specific, Measurable, Achievable, Realistic, and Time-bound. You're probably not reading about SMART goal setting for the first time, and while I agree with that approach, I also find that SMART goals tend to focus on *what* is to be achieved and *when*; however, the *how and why* part of the equation is often left unaddressed. The how and why are critical.

Look at Figure 13-2, Goal Planning, which shows how to address these factors at every level.

Goal Planning

Individual Goal Planning Worksheet				
Goal/Category	Financial	Customer Perspective	Internal Process	Learning & Growth
Benefits of Achieving Goal				
Major Obstacles to Overcome to Achieve Goal				
Skills and Knowledge Required to Achieve Goal				
People, Companies, Groups Who Can Help Me				
Plan of Action				
Completion Date				

Team/Dept. Goal Planning Worksheet

Goal/Category	Financial	Customer Perspective	Internal Process	Learning & Growth
Benefits of Achieving Goal				
Major Obstacles to Overcome to Achieve Goal				
Skills and Knowledge Required to Achieve Goal				
People, Companies, Groups Who Can Help Me				
Plan of Action				
Completion Date				

Company Goal Planning Worksheet

Goal/Category	Financial	Customer Perspective	Internal Process	Learning & Growth
Benefits of Achieving Goal				
Major Obstacles to Overcome to Achieve Goal				
Skills and Knowledge Required to Achieve Goal				
People, Companies, Groups Who Can Help Me				
Plan of Action				
Completion Date				

Figure 13-2

Written goals are only the beginning of expectation setting. Managers at every level must constantly review their direct reports' goals and continue to focus on how to achieve them, making the review of the "how" as objective and quantifiable as possible. The more quantifiable any goal or metric is—along with the steps needed to achieve it—the easier it is to be clear about expectations and achievements.

In addition to goal setting, accountability is a key component of setting clear expectations. At Midcourse Advisors, we help our clients by using this weekly accountability worksheet that positively impacts results by clarifying expectations:

Weekly Accountability Worksheet

Name: _____

Partner: _____

Date: _____

Rate yourself on a scale of 1–10 for the week.
1 = Terrible / 10 = Great

1	2	3	4	5	6	7	8	9	10

What HIGH-IMPACT/INCOME tasks have I accomplished this week?

What HIGH-IMPACT/INCOME tasks do I intend to accomplish next week?

What is ONE specific HIGH-IMPACT or HIGH-INCOME task
my accountability partner can help me with?

_____

What top 3 things have happened this week that I feel really good about?

_____

_____

What did I set out to achieve this week but didn't? How can I correct this?

_____

_____

What specific challenges do I need help with? (And who can help me?)

_____

_____

What new insights or realizations have I had this week?

_____

_____

Figure 13-3

ASSIGNMENT	Time to pause and put what you learned to work. Meet with your team and let them pick accountability partners, then implement it. You can download a template at www.midcourseadvisors.com/growlikeapro.

CLIENT EXPECTATIONS

Just as important as it is to set clear expectations with team members, it is critical to do the same with your clients. You may not think you have the same level of influence over clients as you do with team members because you lack specific authority, but I disagree. I believe you can and should influence a client's behavior by setting clear expectations for the client as a valuable partner and you as the service provider. Let me explain how I've accomplished this.

First, I sold with integrity. I was never the most articulate, smooth-talking salesperson. When I started as an account manager, my organizational and executional skills far surpassed my presentation and influencing skills. I was only successful because I focused on building trust, not overselling, and then making sure my teams and I delivered on everything promised.

Part of this key communication is to set expectations regarding client behaviors required to ensure success. It is important to be very clear in written form about the impact of their noncompliance or lack of cooperation. For example, if you need client approval on certain project milestones and the client isn't available or can't make a decision, you can't really be held accountable for a rigid timeline. Communicate this from the outset.

Surveys can be another way to set expectations with your clients, but my suggested approach to client surveys turns the entire process on its head. Let's face it—we're all inundated with surveys after some action, and we don't really want to take the time to complete a survey for a car service, a plumber's repair, etc. You know what I'm talking about. I'm never certain how the collected data is used, and asking *after* service delivery is completely reactionary. It is also meaningless—if my experience was so poor, I'm never using that provider again.

REAL-WORLD EXAMPLES

During my time at USI, Beazer Homes was one of my clients, and together with our contacts at the corporate level, we created a survey we dubbed the Customer Success Scorecard (CSS).

It was designed to generate a top score only if we exceeded all expectations, both qualitatively and quantitatively. Now here's the catch: we gave them the CSS in advance, explained how we'd created it, and stressed that we wanted them to have the best customer service experience ever. We went on to explain that we were presenting it at the start with the goal of achieving a perfect ten on each and every performance category. We reiterated that as we moved through the process, they should refer to the CSS, and if they felt at any point we were not earning a ten, they should contact us immediately so that we could address and correct right then and there.

This had a huge impact on all stakeholders. It showed we were proactive and cared about clients with a very high bar set for customer service. We set a very clear expectation about quality and we delivered, rarely receiving a concerned call that we were not performing at the ten level. The key to success wasn't the vehicle, the CSS. It was the approach—setting clear expectations from the start.

Without clear expectations in place, both for your team and your clients, a project will launch without a good flight plan. You may know your place and time of departure but know nothing about the arrival—never an enviable place to be, and chances are excellent you'll never arrive at your intended destination. Being proactive and setting clear expectations works, and you can take that to the bank . . . literally.

Figure 13-3 is the CSS we used with Beazer Homes. Yes, by today's standards, it is a bit archaic, but that's not the point. The point is it was used proactively, not reactively.

Customer Success Scorecard

Please reply to all applicable questions. We appreciate the feedback as we strive to continuously improve to meet your needs.		
Project Location	**Beazer Point Contact**	**Date**

Questions	Grade (1–5) 5 is best, 1 is worst
When engaged by your VP, was USI responsive in contacting you?	
When first in contact, did USI review the process with you?	
Did USI keep in touch, communicate well, and keep you informed throughout the process?	
Did USI provide a review and analysis of the short-listed proposals?	
Was USI thorough in its due diligence, resulting in a good understanding of the local market?	
Did USI identify suitable alternative locations for your consideration?	
If applicable, how would you rate the performance of the local field broker?	
Did USI provide leadership and insight for optimal negotiations?	
Was the USI team enjoyable to work with?	
Overall Score	
Signature	
Comments	

Figure 13-4

Today, companies often use scorecards with their clients. Many are online, which is convenient and accessible for clients. At the same time, you can analyze the information more easily. SurveyMonkey is the most popular tool used right now, but there are many other applications available.

There are a number of different customer metrics to benchmark and monitor customer feedback. The most common are:

1. Net Promoter Score (NPS®): NPS measures customer loyalty. Simply, it measures how likely it is a customer would recommend your products and/or services to another friend or colleague. It is the most common feedback survey metric—easy to understand, quick to complete, and gives a big-picture gauge of customer loyalty.
2. CSAT (Customer Satisfaction): CSAT evolved from market research surveys and is easy to understand, simple to use, and can be rich in insight. It measures how a customer would rate their overall satisfaction with the goods/services received.
3. CES (Customer Effort Score): CES focuses on the effort your customer needs to put in to interact with you. The theory is, the lower the effort, the happier the customer.

Before collecting any customer feedback, it's important to determine your goal to ensure you're getting the data you need. Your survey questions and timing could be drastically different, depending on what you're trying to measure.

While it's useful to collect feedback and understand your customers, it only makes an impact if you put the data to use. Customer feedback can help drive your product road map, motivate your employees, and increase market share.

Organizations that are customer-centric have buy-in from every department, including the executive team. They understand that one department is not responsible for great customer service, but that relevant information must be provided throughout the organization to make better decisions.

This is why dashboards are useful at every level. Using an analytics dashboard, you can:

- Track progress against key customer experience and operational targets.
- Understand customer behavior, identify friction points, and prioritize the key drivers of satisfaction.
- Coach teams with data and real-time metrics.
- Predict customer behavior and drive customer loyalty.

To find additional information about securing and using customer feedback, including systems to consider and templates to download, go to www.midcourseadvisors.com/growlikeapro.

PRO POINTERS

- Setting clear expectations sets the stage for success, and you'll find even more success with transparency about how the whole picture fits together and how every department and every team member can contribute.

- In defining expectations, explain the alignment, measurement, and reward.

- SMART goals are fine, but you'll find they're much more attainable when you address the "how and why" part of the equation.

- Use the Accountability Worksheet to clarify expectations. Remember to set clear expectations with clients as well.

- Never oversell, or you're setting yourself up for failure from the start.

- If you survey clients, follow my example rather than being reactionary.

- Gain customer feedback and employ score cards, but be certain to put the data to use.

Chapter 14

ORGANIZE THOUGHTFULLY

"Great things in business are never done by one person. They're done by a team of people."

—*Steve Jobs*
Founder of Apple

You've probably noticed that I often use "team member" rather than "employee" or even "associate." There's a sound reason for that—I value teamwork, and I know that it takes teamwork to truly inspire and sustain growth. As I explained in the last chapter, you cannot overlook "how" things are done, and "how" things are done almost always relies on teamwork.

With a thoughtfully organized team, members can focus on the good of the organization and their teammates instead of only focusing on themselves and the job they do. After all, it must all fit together to move your organization toward extraordinary growth. Consider any team sport that you may enjoy. Whether it's football, baseball, basketball, rugby, soccer, or lacrosse, there are various positions involved. A team full of quarterbacks will lack needed blocking to advance and will never play defense well, if at all.

There are also different personalities and skill sets needed to fill the various positions on every team, in sports and in your business. Typically, a big, hulking 250-pound guy will be a better blocker than a running back, who needs greater quickness and agility. Sure, the running back moves the ball down the field, but without blocking . . . well, you get the picture.

The same thing is true in any organization. Salespeople may be closing deals, but they won't be able to do so without those who actually provide the service and the back-office professionals who handle the accounting and necessary administrative work. In business, as in sports, certain personality types fill certain roles better, and this diversity of personality types is the foundation of every well-organized team.

Recognizing this, I attended training to become a Certified TetraMap Facilitator, and this certification enables me to better serve my own clients in their team-building efforts. TetraMap is a methodology using nature as a metaphor to identify different personality types and better understand how people think and act. When you know your style and adjust your communication based on knowing the styles of others, you can be a far more effective leader or teammate. What I like about TetraMap is its simplicity compared to Myers-Briggs, DISC, or other tools.

The TetraMap methodology uses a tool to determine your most prominent personality type. These include:

TetraMap Personality Types

Personality Type	Characteristics
Earth	Firm. Focuses on getting things accomplished.
Air	Clear. Focuses on performing high-quality work.
Water	Calm. Seeks collaboration and team dynamics.
Fire	Visionary. Seeks new thoughts and opportunities.

Figure 14-1

Each of us exhibits elements of all four types. For example, I am primarily a Fire/Earth person who prefers new ideas and getting things done. But when I encounter a Water, I know I need to be a bit more team-oriented and dial up that part of my disposition. When I am working with an Air, I need to be more prepared to explain the process and have a checklist.

As in nature, all elements are necessary. If all we had on our team were Fire people, we'd have a lot of great ideas flowing every day, but nothing would be accomplished. Similarly, if we only had Water people, we'd all work well together, but not have any direction or visionary ideas to really grow the company. A team filled with Air people will be exacting but may not collaborate well and may execute perfectly—on all the wrong things.

It is key that you hire and form teams that contain different personality types, so you can benefit from varying perspectives and ways of getting things done. When you organize thoughtfully, you are greatly improving your chances for exponential growth.

Finally, as you organize, you should think about how employees on the team are developed. Do you have mentors and mentees so those more experienced team members can share their knowledge and help others? Do you have people on the team who can operate effectively in multiple roles, like a player-coach?

To get more information about using TetraMap, contact us at www.midcourseadvisors.com.

PRO POINTERS

- Value teamwork! It is the key to getting things done and growing.

- Every team needs a combination of skill sets and personality types.

- The TetraMap approach enables you to more easily identify personality types than other assessment tools.

- Any cohesive team must always have a combination of personality types.

Chapter 15

CREATE AN ENVIRONMENT THAT EMBRACES POSITIVE CONFLICT

"Courage is what it takes to stand up
and speak. Courage is also what it
takes to sit down and listen."

—*Winston Churchill*
Prime Minister

In most companies, there are vocal leaders and those who follow. While certainly everyone plays a role and not everyone can be a leader, everyone should have a voice. You want to encourage and allow people to make mistakes and speak up.

There are a number of reasons to welcome everyone's voice, and they are all meaningful and impactful to a successful company.

First, most nonmanagement employees are the ones who interact with customers, suppliers, and partners each and every day. They see what is and isn't working and what should be done to either fortify or improve any situation.

Second, team members can also be at the forefront of innovation.

They have unique skill sets and points of view that can lead to original and creative thinking. When team members know that mistakes are allowed, and possibly even encouraged, they are more likely to experiment with new approaches, and innovation is often the result. If there is fear of making a mistake, people will not venture away from the established way of doing things and will stick to the "it's the way we've always done things" mentality. That mindset is a growth killer.

As a result, as leaders, you need to create an environment that embraces discussion, agreement, disagreement, and even conflict. That doesn't mean everyone has the same vote, but everyone is heard. Wallflowers and "yes men/women" will never enable your business to grow.

When you host a meeting, you need to listen to everyone who has something to offer before you speak. You need to encourage participation and applaud input, whether it is positive or negative.

That's not always so easy, as leaders often are pressed for time, have a strong sense of purpose, and may be the smartest or most experienced person in the room. Regardless, a higher title doesn't always translate into the best ideas. It simply means that person has more responsibility as the shepherd for the organization as a whole. In fact, most high-performing, driven people promoted into leadership must now fundamentally change their approach. Many of the paradigms that led to their promotion into leadership won't make them successful as leaders.

According to the book *Multipliers*, by Liz Wiseman, the best leaders make everyone smarter. As she rightly points out, organizations tend to find smart, talented people and then promote them into management. That doesn't mean they know how to manage.

The best managers and leaders provide direction, share vision, ask questions, review with a critical but noncriticizing eye, trust that they have the right people in place, and then get out of their way.

The managers' job then becomes one of removing roadblocks to their teams' successes, whatever those may be. Then they challenge the individuals to do more, be better, asking them to rethink how they accomplished the task at hand by asking "what-if" questions.

REAL-WORLD EXAMPLES

While president at IEM, I made a big mistake from which I learned an extremely valuable lesson.

One month, I held our leadership meeting in which each leader presented his/her current initiatives, secured feedback, and provided support.

I don't recall the sequence, but when our CFO presented, he was way off base on the financial assumptions he forecast.

Rather than letting him finish his presentation and share his point of view, I interrupted and corrected him. I justified this, as leader of the company, I needed to make sure we were all on track and weren't wasting time. These assumptions could lead to poor decisions and outcomes, which were my responsibility to proactively address.

Right away, I knew I had done something very wrong when I saw his body language. He answered me very defensively and then slumped in his chair.

I quickly recognized that in this meeting, I had not created create an environment that welcomed ideas, good or bad, and given people credit for their effort and point of view.

Afterward, I apologized to all the leaders in the room and then individually to the CFO for my mistake. Fortunately, I had been a decent leader up until then, so I was able to get past this incident pretty quickly, and I vowed never to do that again.

Since then, I have focused on running my meetings differently to encourage dialogue and conflict without consequence.

First, I share the podium. Rather than leading the meeting each time, I give the floor to others to lead. This chair is rotated and communicated in advance. Given some common elements for each meeting, the chair sets the agenda and run the meeting as the person sees fit. This approach gives each team member an opportunity to have a voice and develop a presence in front of peers.

Second, I listen and don't talk until all the others have had their say. What happens is amazing. People aren't afraid to talk. They share opinions. They challenge one another.

Third, I act as a cheerleader. When I do chime in, it is 100 percent without judgment. I applaud any presentation, suggestion, or comment.

The bottom line: if you have a good team, they collectively are usually right. At USI, we secured a new, major account I wasn't in favor of pursuing, but my team convinced me how we could make our desired margins and also how it could enhance our brand. It ended up being a very strong account, one that we would not have secured if I hadn't listened. At IEM, we passed on an opportunity with a major brand name because it would not have been profitable.

Another aspect to consider is how you align operationally. There are many areas in which being transparent and clear is helpful to the team. This includes job descriptions and compensation. Some areas may not require such clarity. This can provide some conflict, but inspire greater outcomes.

One example is geographic responsibility. In situations when your products and services can be delivered from anywhere, there is little reason to have geographic boundaries. This can cause conflict among traditional sales teams, since more than one salesperson or team may be pursuing the same opportunities. However, if someone lives in New York and has relationships in Chicago, why should the person be limited to the Northeast?

The best team members know how to manage through uncertainty and adversity, and control what they can control. As long as the company has systems to manage the effort, like a CRM for sales, then limiting geography may not be necessary.

Healthy conflict is okay, and you want to encourage it. It invites diverse points of view, builds commitment, and helps lead to better decisions. When managed properly, conflict often strengthens relationships. It's okay to be assertive, provided it's done respectfully. Be "necessarily honest" as opposed to "brutally honest." Healthy conflict always focuses on the issue, not the person, and seeks understanding, not necessarily agreement.

PRO POINTERS

- Encourage team members to make mistakes and speak up.

- Team members are often at the forefront of innovation. When they know mistakes are allowed, they're more likely to experiment with new ideas and approaches.

- While everyone doesn't have the same vote, everyone should be heard. Trust you have the right people in place, and then get out of the way.

- Consider sharing the podium and let others run the meeting.

Chapter 16

YOU ARE THE EXAMPLE

"Leadership is about making others better
as a result of your presence and making
sure that impact lasts in your absence."

—*Sheryl Sandberg*
COO of Facebook

According to the Congressional Budget Office, income for the top 1 percent is set to increase by 17 percent from 2016 to 2021, or an average of $200,000 per year.

Employees know leaders earn the most and accept it. Leaders have the most responsibility and take the most risk. But team members also want to feel as if they are treated fairly, whether it is related to compensation or other work aspects.

Dan Price, founder/CEO of Gravity Payments, understands this mindset. He decided to increase his employees' minimum wage for full-time teammates to $70,000 per year, or a 57 percent increase from $30,000.

This enables employees to buy homes, pay off debt, start families, save for retirement, provide for their kids' college, and take vacations. With improved happiness, employees perform. In fact, from 2015 to 2019, this business grew by over 300 percent.

Eric Bieniemy, current offensive coordinator of the Kansas City Chiefs, also gets it. Each week during the season, he invests the time to memorize the two-hundred-plus plays the team has designed for its upcoming opponent.

When asked why he does that and what value it brings, Bieniemy explained, "Football is about inspiring young men to execute as one. To do this, our players need to be really familiar with the details and be able to recall and implement them seamlessly. I need to set the example. Though I have access to all the plays on a card, by memorizing, I can help my team make better and faster decisions."

Leaders leave their mark in so many ways, not the least of which is providing the vision and making critical decisions. They set the tone for the organization, which ultimately affects the culture and the brand. Truly impactful leaders demonstrate behaviors that the rest of the team will want to emulate. The best way to lead is to model the behaviors we want to see in others.

One of the reasons USI grew to become an Inc. 500 company was because our leadership dug in and did everything we would ask anyone else to do—and I mean everything. We came in early and stayed late. It was not beneath senior management to run to the store for supplies if we ran out. Early on, we shared rooms on business trips to cut expenses and drove colleagues to the airport instead of using a car service. We helped bind proposals and ensured they met our quality standards. The message it sent to the team was that we were willing to do whatever it took, and we were clearly walking the walk. No matter what title was on our business card, we set the example for behavior standards.

> When your business is new, show your team
> that you're working as hard as they are. Come
> in early and stay late. Run out for supplies.
> Do whatever the team members are doing.

As a leader, being effective can easily trump being efficient. Setting the right example depends on your own mindset. For me, my credo is "Touch the Post," which developed during my days on the track team as a long-distance runner. I had a favorite route I ran on weekends that included a long hill that I needed to crest, run down, and then run back up. At the bottom of the hill was a post, and of the hundreds of times I ran that route, I always ran down and touched the post rather than turning around early at the top of the hill. Today, my well-ingrained credo translates to don't take shortcuts, do everything with my best effort.

REAL-WORLD EXAMPLES

I have had great leadership examples throughout my own career—people who exhibited behaviors that were impactful and whom I wanted to emulate because I saw the benefit to the team.

Ed McLaughlin, USI's founder, taught me the value of being effective over efficient. We worked on numerous proposal drafts together. Ed cared immensely about the importance of every written word. He wanted to illustrate such thoughtfulness and creativity that it would make USI stand out as the differentiated and natural choice.

Ed found it more effective to write his thoughts on a notepad prior to translating to a word processor. For each proposal, there were dozens and dozens of cross-outs and rewrites. We would stay up until the middle of the night reviewing and editing. It would have been far easier to not make as many corrections and use a word processor, but this wasn't about efficiency; it was about effectiveness.

People who work with me ask me how I learned to be so thorough. I tell them it's all due to Ed.

Rick Bertasi, president of USI, was another such mentor. He had great determination and immense confidence in our ability to succeed even when we were the underdogs. It made me and my teams believe we could do anything. Rick and I both liked to work out and often trained together. I once had the opportunity to toast him and proudly shared, "Rick is the guy who during the mountain-biking section of an adventure race would applaud you if you were ahead of the pack, push you to do better if you were in the middle, and give you a tow if you were in the back of the pack." He did exactly the same thing in the office with our team. As a result, I try to embrace Rick's behavior and work every day to emulate that.

If you've been fortunate to have had some great leadership mentors, I'm sure you can relate to these stories. If you're struggling to think of any, it's time to get some. No matter where you are in your business or your career—corner office or still climbing through middle management—it is never too late. Determine where you need to improve and find someone who does well what you need to learn and ask for help.

While it's important to model great behaviors and have a positive influence and impact on others, this cannot occur in a vacuum. You must pay attention and understand that everyone has different needs and methods by which they want to be encouraged and coached. The mentoring, support, and compensation models that work for one team member may not work for another. Some live for their families and some are constantly engaged in their work 24/7. Some need constant challenges, or they get bored easily. Some need more feedback. You must engage with your team to determine what they want to achieve and how they want to live their lives.

Once you understand what makes people tick, model the appropriate behaviors and empower them to perform and grow!

PRO POINTERS

- Effective leaders prove that they are willing to do whatever it takes by rolling up their sleeves and walking the walk.

- Choose being effective over being efficient. It's ideal to be both, but if you can't, choose the former. You'll have greater impact.

- Consider the leaders and mentors in your life and career and the behaviors that they exhibited that are worth emulating.

- It's never too late to have a mentor. Identify the areas in which you wish to improve, find an expert, and ask.

- Understand what makes your team tick in order to be a mentor to the team and the people on it.

- Always pay it forward.

DEVELOP THE RIGHT PARTNERSHIPS

Chapter 17

THE RIGHT PARTNERS CAN LAUNCH YOU FORWARD

"In a very real sense, there are only two roles in organizations: customers and suppliers. Everybody functions simultaneously in both roles, whether inside or outside the organization. The essence of good business, therefore, is the quality of the relationship between customer and supplier."

—Stephen Covey
Business Leader and Author

When most companies start out or want to grow beyond their current size, they have several paths to achieve such growth.

One primary way is to grow organically based on the internal resources at your company and the relationships you have or seek to establish. This isn't a bad route for those who wish to have measured growth they can implicitly control.

For a company to expand appropriately and quickly, it is important to establish partnership arrangements with partners that can extend your company's capabilities and reach. You want contractual alignments with third parties that, when done properly, enhance the value of both partners.

A strategic partnership is a mutually beneficial arrangement between two separate companies that don't directly compete with one another. They can focus on marketing, supply chain, integration, technology, and finances.

Companies have long engaged in strategic partnerships to enhance their offers and offset costs. The concept is that two are better than one, and by combining resources, partner companies add advantages for both companies through the alliance.

The Business Model Canvas (BMC) detailed in Chapter 1 highlights Channels or Path to Customers as one of its key categories.

Trademarks? Some examples with which you may be familiar include Starbucks's in-store coffee shops at Barnes & Noble bookstores, HP, and Disney's ultra-hi-tech Mission: SPACE attraction, and Nokia and Microsoft's joint partnership agreement to build Windows Phones.

Just as important as knowing what strategic partnerships can offer, it is key to recognize that they are not a panacea for your hopes and dreams. It is actually an opportunity to make the effort to ensure the partnership works, because often, they don't.

REAL-WORLD EXAMPLES

A personal example is one of my clients, Yardarm Technologies. This company created a unique product to help law enforcement be more accountable to its communities and vice versa. The product was a sophisticated sensor that fit into the grip part of a firearm that records when a firearm is removed from its holster, turns on a body camera automatically, and provides evidence such as key forensic data when a bullet has discharged.

While Yardarm had some key early adopters of its products and services, it did not have the resources or reach to sustain, much less grow the company.

As a result, the company partnered with other businesses in its value chain. These were companies that Yardarm's products and services complemented and had similar sets of customers, including manufacturers of the firearms, body cameras, and other radio connecting technologies.

One of the best relationships it established was with Motorola. Motorola incorporated Yardarm in its suite of products, providing reach in the United States and across the globe the company would not have enjoyed otherwise.

While Yardarm did well in establishing partnerships, such as the one with Motorola, the company had some tough lessons along the way. Yardarm management thought it had such good rapport with its partners and that its product was so differentiated, it would almost sell itself. Guess what, it didn't.

As a result, it updated its agreements to incorporate incentives and training for the sales teams or minimums the partners would commit to selling. Once in place, the company was able to take fuller advantage of this reach.

GET CONNECTED

To find good partners, you should connect with people and firms in your industry. Go to trade shows. Talk to customers about other firms from which they procure goods and services. Ask your existing providers and suppliers, such as legal, accounting, and other firms, to connect you to potential partners in their networks. You can't connect without getting out there.

Key questions to ask when you're looking for a partner include:

- Will the company help you and your company sell more product or reduce costs?
- Will the partnership have senior-level sponsorship and visibility?
- Will the partner fit culturally?
- Does it have the resources to execute?
- Will it invest in the relationship and will this be a priority for the business?

- Will the partner benefit as well?

Essential elements for a partnership agreement should include:

- A written agreement
- Negotiated deal with someone who can contract on behalf of the business
- Detailed description of both parties' obligations in the written agreement
- Specific payment terms in agreement.
- Termination clause in contract
- Dispute resolution specified
- Agreement to keep terms and conditions confidential

To me, the absolute crucial part of the agreement is item #3 about the rights and obligation of each party. Make sure each party is set up to succeed, as win-lose partnerships don't work.

Work with an attorney to draft any partnership agreements. There is too much at stake to have a sloppy contract.

For a sample partnership agreement, go to my website www. midcourseadvisors.com/growlikeapro.

PRO POINTERS

- To grow faster, consider a strategic partnership that enhances the value of both organizations by increasing offers and sales, reducing costs, or both.

- Look for partners that complement your own products/services and customer base.

- To find good partners, get connected. Go to trade shows. Talk to customers and providers. Be sure you can explain why the partnership would be beneficial to both companies.

- Spelling out the details is a critical component of a successful agreement. And don't leave it to chance. Consult an experienced partnership attorney.

MANAGE FINANCES

Chapter 18

RAISE CAPITAL

"If you come in with a theory, and a plan and no data, and you're one of the next thousand, it's going to be far, far harder to raise money."

—Marc Andreessen
American Entrepreneur,
Investor, and Software Engineer

Raising capital to start a business can be a daunting process, especially for entrepreneurs who have a great idea but have never run a business. For established businesses, accessing additional capital to fund other opportunities for growth can be just as difficult.

Running a business requires a great deal of capital. Financial capital consists of assets, securities, and, of course, cash. Having access to cash can mean the difference between companies expanding or being left behind. The truth is, you can't move forward and can't pass "Go" without cash.

There are a number of trade-offs that most business leaders don't fully understand until they jump into the pool. By the time they do, it can be a really good decision, or sometimes, it is too late to see they've chosen the wrong option.

So, the big question is, how can you raise the capital you need to keep your company going and fund future projects? And what options are available?

Assuming the capital isn't allocated by the company from ongoing operations, the two primary choices for business leaders are debt and equity. Companies borrow capital as debt in the form of short- and long-term loans and repay them with interest.

Equity is raised by issuing common and preferred stock and through retained earnings, but does not require repayment.

Before we get into the types of capital and the amount you may need, it's important to understand that getting investors is not a growth strategy; getting customers is. Consider the advice of *The Shark Tank's* Mark Cuban: "Go it alone as long as you can." As he explains, raising money is more of an obligation than an accomplishment, and you're responsible to whomever loaned the money. Instead, you want to control the vision and future of the company you've launched.

Additionally, whether it's a new business or an expanding one, you will always need to justify the investment. Put yourself in the shoes of potential investors. They're going to want to know what return they can expect on their investment. Be certain you have your proverbial ducks in a row, and we'll cover the aspects of a business plan later in this chapter.

That said, now let's talk about ways to raise capital and determine the amount. Many business owners and executives try to minimize the amount they require because they are optimistic about their offering and want to minimize the risk optics to debtors or equity holders. This is usually a mistake because expansion often takes longer and requires more capital than expected.

Having to go back to the well for additional capital is far harder than the initial ask, so make sure you have adequate capital to develop your product/service and a long enough runway to gain enough momentum to be self-funded.

Note, most companies secure multiple rounds of funding over time, but for each round, there should be adequate capital to achieve the desired goals.

DEBT

Entrepreneurs and owners of new businesses almost always use personal debt to initially fund their companies. Some position their initial investment in the business as a loan to be repaid over time. Others may borrow the cash value of their personal life insurance policies. These funds are usually available at a relatively low interest rate. Still others borrow money against the equity in their personal residences. This can be risky since the residence is used as collateral. Finally, some use personal credit cards to fund their businesses. Owners pay higher interest rates, which increases the risk of accumulating more debt.

For those requiring additional funds beyond personal debt, conventional debt is borrowed funds whose principal and interest must be repaid on a predetermined schedule. They can be short term or longer term in nature.

On the positive side, debt is preferred by many owners because it doesn't dilute ownership value. It is also the best way to create leverage as you use the funds to drive a higher return than the interest rate you are paying to the fund source. Debt is often tax deductible, which reduces the overall cost of debt.

On the negative side, it can be challenging to pay the interest on a regular basis, especially in a rising interest rate environment. In addition, debt ranks as a high company liability because owners are required to pay interest before issuing dividends to shareholders. Finally, sources of debt often require collateral, which can be challenging for a fledgling company or an established one with limited assets.

Sources of debt include, but are not limited to, private and public sources.

Private sources include:

- Friends and family

Friends and family are a logical first source of funds. You may get more understanding and favorable terms than from banks or other lenders given your personal relationship. The main challenge with this option is those who lend money may want to get involved in the business, regardless of their experience or skills. In addition, when things don't go well, personal relationships can be strained or even jeopardized. If you're pursuing this route, the business relationship needs to be formalized and documented as with any other third party.

- Banks, including credit unions

Banks and other financial institutions are the next logical choice. They have experience providing business loans.

Credit unions focus on a specific group, such as employees of a company or members of a labor union.

Finance companies generally charge higher interest rates than banks and credit unions. Their loans are typically secured by a specific asset as collateral. They can seize the asset if the business defaults on the loan.

Consumer finance companies make small loans against personal assets.

Commercial finance companies provide small businesses with loans for inventory and equipment purchases.

Finally, insurance companies often make commercial loans. They usually provide payment terms and interest rates comparable to a commercial bank but require a business to have more assets available as collateral.

Public sources include:

- Small Business Administration loans

State and federal governments offer programs that provide funding to promote the formation and growth of small businesses. Many of these programs are managed by the US Small Business Administration (SBA).

The SBA helps small businesses obtain funds from banks and other lenders by guaranteeing loans up to $750,000, to a maximum of 70 to 90 percent of the loan value, for only 2.75 percentage points above the prime lending rate. To qualify for an SBA-guaranteed loan, an entrepreneur must first be turned down for a loan through regular channels.

Finally, Small Business Investment Companies (SBICs) are government-backed firms that make direct loans or equity investments in small businesses. SBICs tend to be less risk-averse than banks, so funds are more likely to be available for start-up companies. Another advantage is that SBICs are often able to provide technical assistance to small business borrowers.

For established businesses, the debt options are essentially the same, but your company's track record demonstrating an ability to repay the debt reduces the risk, providing more favorable terms with more financial institutions able and willing to participate.

The key difference is the ability to establish a line of credit (LOC). A LOC is a floating-rate, revolving loan. It is repayable monthly, like a credit card, but has a reduced interest rate. It's a good option for companies seeking to best manage cash flow to invest in short-term requirements to drive the business forward or pay for goods or services in advance of securing the revenue associated with these goods or services. An example is a clothing manufacturer that must buy the cotton or yarn in advance of making the garments.

Established companies can pay for such items with working cash flow, but may not elect to do so if cash is tight or there are other priorities that need funds.

EQUITY

Equity capital includes funds invested or earned by shareholders. It is different than debt in that equity capital reflects ownership, while debt capital reflects an obligation.

Though, unlike debt, the funds do not need to be repaid, but there is an expectation of a return on investment based on the opportunity the investment may provide and the associated risk. As a result, the cost of equity most often exceeds the cost of debt because the payment is required by law ahead of dividends or return on equity.

Equity capital may come in the following forms:

- Common Stock: Companies sell common stock to shareholders to raise cash. Common shareholders can vote on certain company matters.
- Preferred Stock: This type of stock gives shareholders no voting rights but does grant ownership in the company. These shareholders get paid before common stockholders if the business is liquidated.
- Retained Earnings: These are profits the company has retained over the course of the business's history that have not been paid back to shareholders as dividends.

Equity can be secured in a number of ways.

For newer companies, when still in early idea or prototype form, seed investment may be acquired to supplement any personal debt incurred. This can come from friends and family, individual investors or investment organizations, or companies that provide funding at early stages.

Angel investment organizations or companies provide funding for newer companies that have launched but are still in early development stages.

Accredited investors (those with a certain level of assets and income) provide funding for companies that are typically ready to serve customers and, as required, as the company strives to become profitable.

Venture capital is financing given to start-up companies and small businesses that are seen as having the potential to grow rapidly. Funding usually comes from wealthy investors, investment banks, and any other financial institutions. The investment may not be only financial, it can also be offered via technical or managerial expertise.

Private equity firms invest in or outright purchase established companies they believe are undervalued or have great potential. A cash infusion and leveraging private capital companies' advisors can help drive strong value. They often help streamline operations to increase revenues and profits.

Finally, given the availability of information and reach available on the internet, crowdfunding has become another option for new companies. Investment crowdfunding is a way to source money for a company by asking a large number of backers to each invest a relatively small amount. In return, backers receive equity shares of the company. Normally restricted to accredited investors, the 2015 Jobs Act in the United States allows for a greater scope of investors to invest via crowdfunding once better infrastructure is in place to do so.

Companies seeking crowdfunding typically create a Minimum Viable Product (MVP) and demonstrate demand and/or a unique value proposition. Through crowdsourcing websites or local business events, individual investors can invest in the company and even place advanced orders for the products or services. Investors can become fractional equity owners without having to expend thousands and thousands of dollars. In fact, some require as little as ten dollars.

Crowdfunding has become popular for companies that have created a unique product, such as PrintPen, which is a company that created a portable printer for all materials and surfaces. As of this writing, the company raised over $472,000 from 3,024 backers, or $156 per investor.[12]

For each equity participant listed, the risk-reward varies, but

12   EVEBOT, "PrintPen: Portable Printer for All Materials and Surfaces," Kickstarter project, last updated February 29, 2020, https://www.kickstarter.com/projects/1874428722/printpen-portable-printer-for-all-materials-and-surfaces.

typically, the earlier the investment, the lower valuation and greater return expected.

Equity participants may be passive or active investors, depending on the amount of investment, value added, and the arrangement reached with the company owners.

There are many benefits and drawbacks of engaging with active investors. Active investors provide direction, connections, and cash that can help boost a company's growth prospects. On the other hand, you may sacrifice control and nimble decision-making capability. While passive owners expect a return and ongoing communication regarding progress to achieve that goal, active owners expect ongoing reporting and involvement in decision-making.

REAL-WORLD EXAMPLES

At USI, the company adhered to the "go it alone" advice and was funded by personal debt of the founder. Risk was mitigated by identifying and securing a number of customers before launching, ensuring profitability within the first year.

Additional shareholders, myself included, became invested based on the risk taken joining USI in its infancy as well as the skills and contributions we brought to the company.

The idea of pursuing equity capital was dismissed because management didn't want to yield to any outside control. We didn't want the obligation of reporting nor the potential for investors to alter the vision. This proved to make a big difference in our company, as, culturally, we were a group of aggressive and nimble owners who would not have done well collaborating or answering to others.

With this in mind, USI grew vertically and geographically with client demand. This ensured ongoing growth funding would provide an ROI.

IEM was founded and developed similarly to USI. However, the company was largely acquired by a private equity firm to expand growth possibilities.

My experience with this private equity firm wasn't fruitful. I took over for the founder of an established, successful business after the acquisition with the goal of enhancing the offering and operational capabilities to drive more revenue and profitability. It was part of a larger acquisition with four other companies. We were hitting all our targets, but not all the others were.

I learned multiple lessons at USI and IEM regarding capital raising and have since advised a number of other companies how to navigate this important business requirement.

First, it is vitally important to do your homework. Use the Business Model Canvas as described in earlier chapters to model and plan for your business. This is applicable to new and existing companies.

Second, draft a business plan. This is important, as you can't really demonstrate that you understand the opportunity and challenges if you can't document it. A business plan typically incorporates the following elements:

- Mission statement and/or vision statement so you articulate what you're trying to create
- Description of your company and product or service
- Description of how your product or service is different
- Market analysis of the market you're trying to enter, competitors, where you fit, and what type of market share you believe you can secure
- Description of your management team, including the experience of key team members and previous successes
- Your plan to market the product or service
- Analysis of your company's strengths, weaknesses, opportunities, and threats, which will show that you have considered all opportunities and challenges
- A cash flow statement demonstrating you understand what your needs are now and will be in the future (a cash flow statement also can help you consider how cash flow could impact growth)

- Revenue projections
- Summary/conclusion (this also could be an executive summary at the beginning of the plan)

Third, leveraging the business plan, create a pitch deck. This is important because you can't convince other stakeholders to join the journey if you can't communicate and present it. Sequoia Capital recommends the following elements:

- Company Purpose: Define your company in a single declarative sentence. This is harder than it looks. It's easy to get caught up listing features instead of communicating your mission.
- Problem: Describe the pain of your customer. How is this addressed today and what are the shortcomings to current solutions?
- Solution: Explain your eureka moment. Why is your value proposition unique and compelling? Why will it endure? And where does it go from here?
- Why Now: The best companies almost always have a clear "why now?" Nature hates a vacuum—so why hasn't your solution been built before now?
- Market Potential: Identify your customer and your market. Some of the best companies invent their own markets.
- Competition/Alternatives: Who are your direct and indirect competitors? Show that you have a plan to win.
- Business Model: How do you intend to thrive?
- Team: Tell the story of your founders and key team members.
- Financials: If you have any, please include.
- Vision: If all goes well, what will you have built in five years?[13]

For examples of a business plan and pitch deck, go to www.midcourseadvisors.com/growlikeapro.

---

13 Team Sequoia, "Writing a Business Plan," Sequoia Capital, visited April 13, 2020, https://www.sequoiacap.com/article/writing-a-business-plan/.

After you have completed these three steps, find some customers. Don't incur debt or issue equity yet. Validate your new business expansion plans, secure some additional feedback, and generate some cash flow. Then, you can fund the business plan. Starting and expanding a business well focuses on managing and reducing risk. Taking this approach is the best way manage risk and create the desired results.

Now, you may ask, "What if I only have a minimum viable product/service (MVP) that isn't fully functional and therefore cannot generate new or incremental revenue?"

You need to find ways to engage, add value, and make money. Let me give you an example. There is a company called Wripple that has an app that serves as an online integrator between digital talent and companies with digital marketing needs.

Before the company launched the app, it served a number of clients manually. Wripple was able to secure customers and generate revenue because there was demand for its service from both customer types. These customers were also innovative in that they were able and willing to try it and wait for new services as long as they believed Wripple could ultimately deliver on the app and provide the associated benefits.

The following are do's and don'ts of raising capital:

Do's

- Sharpen your focus on the opportunity at hand.
- Know to whom you are pitching.
- Get a referral to financial sources, such as banks, angel investors, or venture capital firms.
- Have a good advisory board.
- Have good legal counsel.
- Have a strong business plan.
- Have strong references.
- Be specific about funding needs.
- Help the investor envision exit value.

Don'ts

- Avoid unrealistic financial projections.
- Avoid a lack of focus on specific market segments.
- Avoid focusing on proprietary technology.
- Avoid focusing beyond twelve months.
- Avoid dismissing competition.

Now that we have learned about raising capital with a better perspective about how to accomplish this, let's move on to capital budgeting.

PRO POINTERS

- Access to cash is often the difference between a business that thrives and grows and one that closes up shop.

- Go it alone as long as you can to maintain control of your vision and business.

- Debt and equity are the ways to raise capital, and each has its benefits and detriments.

- The most common mistake is underestimating how much you need, and it's more difficult to return for additional funding than for the initial ask.

- Lending sources for debt can be private (personal, friends/family, financial institutions) or public (Small Business Administration loans, Small Business Investment Companies).

- Equity capital comes from stock (common or preferred) or retained earnings.

- Although equity does not require a specific payback (as debt does), investors certainly expect a positive return, and those investors may be passive or active. Understand that active investors are going to want a say in decision-making and operations.

- Successfully navigating capital raising requires:
  - Business Model Canvas,
  - business plan,
  - pitch deck,
  - and ideally, customers before you launch.

- Go to www.midcourseadvisors.com/growlikeapro for examples of a business plan and pitch deck.

Chapter 19

CAPITAL BUDGETING

"A debt problem is, at its core,
a budgeting problem."

—Natalie Pace
Author of The ABCs of Money

Once you have secured capital, it is critical to know how to use and manage it to achieve growth and drive expected returns.

You should be aware that not all capital is intended to be utilized and spent immediately. Therefore, you must prioritize the spending and regularly evaluate its use, typically annually.

The natural starting point for prioritization is your business plan, where investment drives associated cash flow.

Capital budgeting is the selection of projects that can have the most impact to the company. Those selected are expected to generate a return that enables the company to continue to grow while fulfilling its debt obligations and generating wealth for shareholders. Capital budgeting is significant because it creates both ownership and accountability for selected projects. The economic feasibility and profitability of a project should be carefully evaluated and measured.

To value these project opportunities, there are two key variables: the rate of return and the ease of implementation. If the return is high, but the timeline to secure the value is long and it taxes the organization from achieving other objectives, it may not be prioritized as highly. Alternatively, easily implementable projects with low returns may not be a project focus either.

> Understand the importance of capital budgeting. It is the selection of projects that can have the most impact to the company.

The rates of return selected help determine if a project proves to be profitable. Most common methods include the payback period, internal rate of return, and net present value.

PAYBACK PERIOD

The payback period (PB) measures how long it takes to pay back the investment before any return is achieved.

For example, if you invested $1 million in goods and services to launch a new brand and that brand was expected to generate $200,000 per year in net profits, the payback period would be five years. Those investments with a shorter payback period are preferred to those with longer payback periods.

Investment	Year 1	Year 2	Year 3	Year 4	Year 5
-$1,000,000	$200,000	$200,000	$200,000	$200,000	$200,000

The payback measurement is typically associated with liquidity. With limited resources, until payback on a project is achieved, you can't invest in other projects.

The payback period is easily calculable and understood, two additional benefits to this measurement.

INTERNAL RATE OF RETURN

The internal rate of return (IRR) is expected financial return on an investment. It is a percentage that is represented by the discount rate that results in a net present value of zero.

Given their inverse relationship, when the discount rate increases, the net present value decreases and vice versa. This means that when the expected cash flows are less, the return expectation is higher.

From a decision standpoint, the IRR needs to be compared to the cost of capital, which is the rate of return that could have been earned by putting the same money into a different investment with equal risk. It is the weighted average of the expected debt and equity returns.

The decision criterion is as follows:

IRR > cost of capital = accept project

IRR < cost of capital = reject project

For example, as seen below, if a company wishes to make an investment outflow of $1.5 million and the resulting cash inflows are $400,000 in each year 1 to 5, the IRR is 10 percent. If the cost of capital is less than 10 percent, you would accept the project.

Investment	Year 1	Year 2	Year 3	Year 4	Year 5
-$1,500,000	$400,000	$400,000	$400,000	$400,000	$400,000

The IRR is useful, as it gives business owners a useful measure to compare projects on an apples-to-apples basis and is a determinant of the company's overall capital structure.

NET PRESENT VALUE

The net present value (NPV) is today's dollar value of all expected after-tax cash flows discounted at the cost of capital.

The NPV is a well-utilized measure because it demonstrates the expected profitability of a project.

The decision criterion is as follows:

NPV > 0 = accept project

NPV < 0 = reject project

For example, per below, if you had a project that had cash flows of a $3 million outgoing investment followed by inflows of $750,000 per year for five years at a discount rate of 8 percent, the NPV would be $671,000. This project would therefore be accepted.

Investment	Year 1	Year 2	Year 3	Year 4	Year 5
-$3,000,000	$750,000	$750,000	$750,000	$750,000	$750,000

You can also compare this result with other projects. For example, a project with an NPV of $771,000 would be favored over the $671,000 NPV project.

Capital budgeting is imperative. You can use one or all the measures as long as you use them consistently. The capital budgeting process and methods I've described are fundamental to evaluating projects. The key is how these measurements are reviewed, measured, communicated, and addressed.

REAL-WORLD EXAMPLES

At both USI and IEM, we evaluated capital projects and created a budget for them. As projects were implemented, we tracked results against forecasted return on a monthly basis and on a daily basis for those working directly on the projects themselves.

We created visibility and accountability through transparency.

We had video displays in our offices that listed key projects/initiatives and how they were tracking in real time both quantitatively and qualitatively. As part of our human resources initiatives, we aligned each team member's expected contributions to specific projects to their performance review.

As a result, senior management was able to review the overall progress and make major adjustments when and where necessary. But the ability to tackle issues that could positively or negatively impact returns was best addressed with team members working on the projects directly in the field.

My suggestion is that you make capital budgeting and measurement a part of your company's culture. After all, you can't change your diet for a short period of time and hope to have good long-term results. Capital budgeting works much the same way.

PRO POINTERS

- Not all capital that you raise must be used and spent immediately.

- Capital budgeting is the selection of projects that can have the most impact to the company. Use your business plan to prioritize.

- To value opportunities, first consider the rate of return and ease of implementation.

- Rates of return help determine project profitability.

- The most common methods to calculate rate of return are:

  o Payback period
  o Internal rate of return
  o Net present value

- You can use any or a combination of the methods. The key is to use them consistently and make capital budgeting part of your company culture.

Chapter 20

FINANCIAL STATEMENT MANAGEMENT

"Revenue is vanity. Profit is sanity. Cash is king."

—Anonymous

You can be very profitable, yet short on cash. Well, how can that be?

It is actually very simple.

Your profit and loss statement can demonstrate profitability and, as you'll read in Chapter 21 on P&L Management, a strong P&L is critical.

However, the timing of revenue and expenses determines the amount and stability of your cash flow. Simply, if you take in cash or equivalents sooner and pay out cash or equivalents later, you will have better chances at being cash rich.

But, if you have spent money on resources to make a product and deliver the work and then don't receive the cash until later due to payment terms, you will have fewer chances of surviving, much less being cash rich.

If your bank account is $100,000 on the first day of the month and $90,000 on the last day of the month, your cash flow was –$10,000 for the month. Your P&L may show $10,000 profit, however, if you accounted for $100,000 of revenue and $90,000 of expense.

Cash is shown on the Balance Sheet, which shows Assets, Liabilities, and Equity. Cash is a liquid asset. If your company's assets are greater than the liabilities, the equity in your company will grow.

The key to manage finances successfully is understanding the three financial statements and how they connect. Per Figure 20-1, you can see a P&L or Income Statement demonstrates profit as the difference between revenue and expenses. The Cash Flow Statement is the use of cash during a time period in operating, financing, and investing activities. The Balance Sheet is the demonstration of Assets less Liabilities, resulting in Equity at a certain period of time.

What is most important to recognize is how the three statements connect. The P&L Net Income or Profit becomes the starting point for the Cash Flow Statement. Finally, the ending cash from the Cash Flow Statement flows into the Balance Sheet.

In addition, there are two elements to consider to optimize cash flow. They include the P&L and also working capital.

The P&L takes into account the cost of goods sold (COGS), which is the direct cost for making a product or delivering the work. Revenue less COGS equals your gross margin. Gross margin less overhead equals your net profit.

Working Capital for products is Accounts Receivables + Inventory – Accounts Payable.

Working Capital for services is Accounts Receivables + Work in Process – Accounts Payable.

If you have other capital that requires resources, such as buildings and research and development, this also needs to be taken into account.

The primary challenge here occurs with growth. When you grow, you seek increased gross margin without proportionate increases in overheads. But to grow, you need additional working capital, which means you can net less, not more.

As you can see in Figure 20-1, there are three primary financial statements: the Income Statement (or P&L), the Cash Flow Statement, and the Balance Sheet. The Income Statement and Cash Flow Statement demonstrate a period of time (e.g. a particular month), whereas the Balance Sheet is a point in time (e.g. December 31, 20XX). Note that the result from the Income Statement, the Net Income, becomes the starting point for the Cash Flow Statement, and the result from the Cash Flow Statement becomes the input in the Balance Sheet. These amounts all tie together and need to be managed closely to run your business effectively.

Income Statement		
	2019	2018
Revenue	$1,104,786	$1,133,736
Cost of Sales		
Opening inventory	156,657	146,278
Delivery	1,607	1,249
Purchases	740,994	794,101
	899,258	941,628
Closing inventory	159,144	156,657
	740,144	784,971
Gross Profit	364,672	348,765
Operating Expenses (Schedule)	286,817	339,905
Income from Operators	77,855	8,860
Other Income (Expenses)		
Loss on disposal of property, plant, and equipment	--	(387)
Gain on sale of investment	16,149	--
Miscellaneous	(1,101)	337
	15,048	(50)
Net Income Before Tax	92,903	8,810
Income Expense	14,387	--
Net Income	78,516	8,810
(Deficit) - Beginning of Year	(61,350)	(54,160)
Dividends	--	(16,000)
Retained Earnings (Deficit) - End of Year	$17,166	$(61,350)

Cash Flow	
	2019
Cash Flows from Operating Activities	
Net income for the year	**$78,516**
Adjustment for:	
Purchases	17,854
Loss on disposal of property, plant, and equipment	--
Gain on disposal of investment	(16,149)
Cash derived from operations	80,221
Decrease (increase) in working capital items	
Accounts receivable	7,625
Deposits and prepaid expenses	(254)
Inventory	(2,487)
Accounts payable and accrued liabilities	(9,290)
Long-term debt - current portion	25,200
Income tax payable	14,387
Cash flows from operating activities	115,402
Cash Flows from Investing Activities	
Acquisition of property, plant, and equipment	(1,426)
Proceeds from disposal of property, plant, and equipment	--
Proceeds from disposal of investment	61,150
Dividends	--
Cash flows from investing activities	59,724
Cash Flows from Financing Activities	
Advances from (repayments to) shareholder	(180,200)
Acquisition of (replayments of) long-term debt	86,100
	(94,100)
Net Increase (Decrease) in Cash Resources	81,026
Cash (Deficiency) Resources - Beginning of Year	(69,474)
Cash Resources (Deficiency) - End of Year	**$11,552**

Balance Sheet

Current	2019	2018
CURRENT		
Cash	$11,552	$--
Accounts receivable	42,970	50,595
Deposits and prepaid expenses	2,942	2,688
Inventory	159,144	156,657
	216,608	209,940
PROPERTY, PLANT, AND EQUIPMENT (NOTE 2	59,890	76,318
INVESTMENTS	--	45,001
	$276,498	$331,259
Liabilities		
CURRENT		
Bank overdraft	$--	$9,474
Bank loan	--	60,000
Accounts payable and accrued liabilities	82,053	91,343
Long-term debt - current portion	25,200	--
Income tax payable	14,387	--
	121,640	160,817
DUE TO SHAREHOLDER	51,591	231,791
LONG-TERM DEBT	86,100	--
	259,331	392,608
Shareholder's Equity		
STATED CAPITAL	1	1
RETAINED EARNINGS (DEFICIT)	17,166	(61,350)
	17,107	(61,349)
	$276,498	$331,259

Figure 20-1

There are seven levers to improving your cash position. They include:

1. Increase price or volume to increase top line sales.
2. Reduce your direct costs or COGS.
3. Reduce your indirect costs or overhead.
4. Decrease your collection timing.
5. Manage your inventory so it doesn't sit without demand.
6. Reduce supplier costs.
7. Increase supplier payment timing.

Making a small impact to each of these areas can change the trajectory of your business.

The best example is a 5 percent increase in price and a 5 percent reduction in COGS. This represents a 10 percent increase in gross margin. If your gross margin was 25 percent, it would now grow to 27.5 percent. Looking at it another way: Previously, it would require $4.00 of revenue to make $1.00 in gross margin. Now, that same $4.00 will produce $1.10 in gross margin.

ASSIGNMENT	Time to pause and put what you learned to work. Identify which of the seven levers you can practically implement and then do it. You can download a template at www.midcourseadvisors.com/growlikeapro.

Why is this all so important?

If you self-fund, you want to stay afloat and need to know the differences amongst the Balance Sheet, Cash Flow, and P&L statements.

For those who decide to take on some debt, such as a line of credit or loan, you need to know what banks consider when approving financing.

Banks or other financial institutions care about your company's ability and capacity to repay the loan plus interest. If there are doubts, you won't get the loan. Key questions include:

- **How leveraged are you?** Your company's Debt/Equity Ratio is the total debt divided by total equity. A typical financial institution seeks this ratio be lower than 3–4 to 1. This is a balance sheet item.

- **How liquid are you?** This is how much cash you have on hand to pay current liabilities. If you have less than five days' worth of sales in cash, then you may have a liquidity problem that gives the bank heartburn.

- **How are you collecting your receivables or turning your inventory?** You should seek to perform at or above terms that are consistent with your industry.

- **Do you have a track record of profitability? Were you profitable last year?** If you were, that's great. If you weren't, don't bother going to the bank, regardless of the good year you're having now. A bank believes the best indicator of the future is the past.

Scale requires investment. If you and your company have infinite financial resources, you may not have to worry about this. Given most companies aren't that fortunate, they need to make sure they are getting a reasonable return.

While your P&L measures ability to generate income, the Balance Sheet demonstrates liquidity, which is required to maintain and invest in to grow the business.

PUTTING NUMBERS TO IT

There are a lot of ways to measure the health of a business. To best manage a company that wants to scale, you should use the Cash Conversion Cycle (CCC). The CCC measures liquidity risk by representing the number of days a firm's cash remains tied up within the operations of the business. It demonstrates efficiently how the company is managing its working capital and is equal to the time it takes to sell inventory and collect receivables less the time it takes to pay the company's payables. The calculation is:

CCC = Days Inventory Outstanding + Days Sales Outstanding – Days Payable Outstanding

Where

Days Inventory Outstanding = Inventory/Average Daily Cost of Goods Sold

Days Sales Outstanding = Accounts Receivable/Average Daily Sales

Days Payable Outstanding = Accounts Payable/Average Daily Cost of Goods Sold

The Cash Conversion Figure 20-2 is an example to help understand how to calculate and also interpret the Cash Conversion Cycle.

Cash Conversion Chart

	2016	2017	2018
Company A			
Days Sales Outstanding	52.51	52.46	48.65
Days Inventory	27.27	26.12	26.81
Days Payables Outstanding	55.51	57.82	64.37
Company B			
Days Sales Outstanding	19.01	25.66	30.51
Days Inventory	3.26	4.37	6.3
Days Payables Outstanding	74.39	74.54	85.45

Figure 20-2

The Cash Conversion Cycle for Company A for 2016 = 52.51 + 27.27 – 55.51 = 24.27

Figure 20-3 shows Cash Conversion Cycle for both companies for the three years.

	2016	2017	2018
Company A	24.27	20.76	11.09
Company B	-52.12	-44.51	-48.64

Figure 20-3

Company B has negative Cash Conversion Cycle of 44 to 52 days during the three-year period, which suggests an exceptionally good working capital management. It means that it could sell and receive cash from its sales even 44 to 52 days before it actually made payments against its production inputs, which is impressive.

Company A, on the other hand, drastically improved its cash conversion over the three years (i.e. from 24.27 in 2016 to 11.09 in 2018), which suggests significant improvement in efficiency of the company. Still, its working capital management is not as good as Company B.

If you work in a service business, you can use a version of the same calculation. Just focus on cash out to pay for employees, partners, and vendors and cash in from accounts receivables. To measure liquidity, you can also incorporate standard industry calculations such as the Current Ratio, which is Current Assets/Current Liabilities, and the Quick Ratio, which is (Current Assets – Inventory)/Current Liabilities.

PRO POINTERS

- Cash flow and profitability are not the same. It all comes down to timing. Your P&L statement can show profit while your bank statement does not.

- You need to understand how the three financial statements, the P&L, Balance Sheet, and Cash Flow Statement, connect and impact one another.

- Working capital, as well as P&L, is a key component of a healthy company, and growth requires working capital.

- Closely monitor the seven levers that will improve your cash position.

- Understand what financial institutions consider before approving a loan.

- Learn to calculate the Cash Conversion Cycle to understand your working capital management.

Chapter 21

PROFIT AND LOSS MANAGEMENT

"Between calculated risk and reckless
decision-making lies the dividing
line between profit and loss."

—*Charles Duhigg*
Journalist and Author of
Smarter, Faster, Better

Profit and loss management connotes a certain level of leadership and accountability. When you grow into a management role, you are often given P&L responsibility for your team, division, or company. When you apply for a management job, you are likely going to be asked if you have P&L management experience.

Why is P&L management so important?

It's significant because it is the heart of a business's daily financial operations. It is how you utilize the capital you raised to run the company. P&L management focuses on tracking revenue and associated expenses, or all the money that flows in and out of an organization.

In other words, P&L management suggests, "The buck stops here."

From an accounting perspective, some companies manage their P&L on a cash basis in which revenue is acknowledged when the check clears and expenses are incurred when the check is written.

For example, a brewer buys materials to produce a line of beer. It would acknowledge the expense ahead of the revenue, as you have to make the beer before you can sell it.

On the other hand, Generally Accepted Accounting Principles (GAAP) often suggest managing a P&L from an accrual basis. This suggests revenue is acknowledged when services/products are provided and expenses when services/products are consumed. This is meant to match revenue and expenses better.

In the case of the brewer, the revenue and expenses would be acknowledged when an order for beer is completed.

For this chapter, we are going to focus on P&L management on a cash basis, because accrual methodology doesn't always reflect the actual funds in the bank that can be used to run the business. And, as we have stated before, "Cash is king!"

REAL-WORLD EXAMPLES

At USI and IEM, we maximized profits by investing and exploiting higher return opportunities, then managing everything very, very closely. We accomplished this by actually pushing financial responsibility down to the lowest management level, as these team members were often closest to the customer and could see what was required to serve most effectively and efficiently. We then tied incentive compensation to both performance and profits, because team members behave in large part based on how they are rewarded. (They also behave on how they are treated, too, which we've already discussed.)

At USI, our business model incorporated pricing our services on a cost-plus basis. Based on a baselined scope of work, we would benefit from fees and commissions that resulted in 30 percent profit margins, which would have been a good outcome for most any company.

But wait, there's more.

Our contracts were exclusive, so for any services we were contracted to provide, we knew we would be able to serve and benefit from any and all additional opportunities without having to sell or negotiate. If there were new or additional services to be provided that we could offer, we were in an ideal position to win that business as well as we knew the client and had already proven ourselves.

Our view was that if our customers' businesses were expanding, we would benefit. If they were contracting, we would also benefit. As long as there was some type of change occurring, which occurred 95 percent of the time or more, we were very profitable.

As important as the incremental revenue was, it is notable that we didn't need to incur the same level of cost to serve the customer. The reason was that for each client, there was a certain level of fixed cost, including resources and technology, covered by the core contract. Some new investment was naturally required to provide specific expertise, more capacity, or more coverage, but, when managed well, this would enhance financial results.

At IEM, we enjoyed high gross margins (revenue less direct costs). We were able to maintain a robust P&L because most of our resources were lower-cost administrators, so we weren't burdened with high direct costs or operating expenses. As long as we continued to grow as a company, which we did under my watch, we were able to continue to add high-margin business and invest in training for the lower-cost administrators to ensure they were productive and remained as happy and appreciated contributors to the company.

At one client that provided IT services, the company managed the financials only in the C-suite. The result was that the line managers didn't know what the impact of their decisions were, both positively and negatively. That made it tough at the beginning of each new month when they didn't know why their projections were off and had to dig in further to determine what was done at the lower levels. When they changed their approach, magic happened as they employed the right people on the right projects at the right time. This maximized talent and cost and minimized downtime.

TREND MANAGEMENT

As important as it is to understand financial statements and their direct linkages, it is just as critical to be able to view and determine trends.

I worked with an engineering firm that was profitable over time, but didn't really have a good handle on what was happening to them financially on a monthly basis.

We started working together in the fourth quarter of 2018. As you can see, the trend wasn't good. Their profit margin, which is income as a percentage of revenue, averaged 29 percent in the first half of the year and –1 percent in the second half. They didn't recognize this.

2018 Financial Trends

	Jan-18	Feb-18	Mar-18	Apr-18	May-18	Jun-18	Jul-18	Aug-18	Sep-18	Oct-18	Nov-18	Dec-18
Total Income	$533,943	$550,705	$584,562	$440,493	$449,987	$314,243	$389,232	$598,419	$304,201	$433,840	$409,624	$511,152
Total Cost of Sales	$233,956	$195,759	$239,546	$173,607	$133,460	$155,852	$152,843	$198,315	$148,089	$230,688	$173,754	$285,612
Total Expenses	$130,353	$81,755	$150,888	$112,952	$199,821	$151,988	$230,443	$139,135	$389,593	$168,101	$179,418	$236,739
Net Income (Loss)	$169,634	$273,191	$194,127	$154,235	$114,844	$4,542	$5,946	$260,588	$(211,250)	$35,051	$56,452	$(31,673)
Net Income/ Revenue	32%	50%	33%	35%	26%	1%	2%	44%	-69%	8%	14%	-6%

Figure 21-1

So, we broke down their financials in detail and determined that the work a major, long-term client provided suddenly slowed down. Yet, the company's costs didn't reduce in tandem. We focused on driving more consistent revenue with a larger variety of clients in 2019 while holding costs in check. Within three months, the results were positive and much more predictable.

This is the type of analysis that good leaders who want their companies to grow need to do on a monthly basis.

KEY LEVERS

Regardless of how strong your business model is, to properly manage a P&L, there are a number of key levers you can and should employ. These include:

- Pricing: Based on the demand for your product/service, know when to increase and decrease prices. If you have a valuable service/product that is differentiated, you may be able to charge more without giving up volume.
- Payment Terms: Depending on the size and type of customers, employ payment terms to accelerate revenue collection. Get clients to pay on terms and conditions they are used to paying for similar types of products/services so you aren't creating obstacles to getting agreement or payment. This can include discounts for paying early and/or penalties for late payments. Then, make sure your contracts enable you to enforce them.
- Procurement: Leverage relationships with your suppliers on an ongoing basis to achieve discounts and

enhance payment terms. If you can pay less and later while collecting higher fees and collecting them sooner, that is a good recipe for positive cash flow and success.

- Direct Costs: Reduce the cost of creating your product or providing your service by enhancing efficiency and minimizing defects.
- Variable Costs: Manage costs of goods and resources that may not be needed on a full-time basis. Employ contractors who are needed on a nonrecurring basis so you can flexibly remove them from your payroll when not needed.
- Operating Expenses: Also known as overhead, these are any costs you incur to keep your business up and running. These expenses typically include rent, administrative expenses, marketing, salaries, and utilities. Stay lean wherever possible here, making sure the overhead in place directly supports the overall mission. Always compare yourself to industry standards that you can secure from industry trade organizations. For example, most healthy companies spend no more than 5 percent of their gross revenue on rent. If you are spending more, this should be justified or addressed.
- Supply Chain Optimization: Simplify the number of touch points within the supply chain, ensuring that supply meets demand and optimizing inventory and distribution strategies. If your supply chain is simpler, there is less chance for challenges in quality, timeliness, and cost.
- Customer Growth: Sell additional products and services to existing customers, retain those customers, and leverage them to bring in new customers. When this occurs, you become more valuable to your existing clients and your cost of sales goes down.
- Employee Focus: Create an employee-centric culture that enables you to attract and retain the best people and enables them to be most productive and

customer-centric. Every newly hired employee takes time to become productive to drive efficiency and effectiveness that help the top and bottom lines.

- Operational Efficiency: Create standardized processes, embrace technology, and align tactics with overall strategy. If you can focus on the key tasks that can remove bottlenecks and enhance efficiency, you will be far better off.

You should understand that most of these items are within your control. If you manage them closely, your chances of success are far better. Don't overlook saving money—i.e. cost reduction—as a means to improve your P&L. In the cost-reduction approach as depicted in Figure 21-2, you first identify and itemize the potential savings. Next, evaluate those potential amounts by going to market to see what you can save. In the third step, you act, followed by negotiating and finalizing. Finally, you'll enjoy the savings you've realized and see the positive impact it's had on your P&L.

As an example, consider a manufacturer with a maintenance contract. First, it realizes that it is overpaying on the contract (identify). Next, it determines the savings it can generate by changing the contract or the amount of maintenance required (evaluate). The company confirms by sending out requests for new bids (either from its existing or new providers). Then, it negotiates a new contract and realizes its savings.

There are a few key elements in this process. First, you need to quantify in each stage. If you want to save $1 million annually, you likely need three times, or $3 million, in possible savings. This creates an initial target that will naturally reduce as you go through the process (no probabilities needed). In addition, this needs to be time bound, so each stage can track and be captured. Review Figure 21-2, the Savings Reduction Process.

Savings Reduction Process

Identify	Evaluate	Confirm	Negotiate	Realize
Savings initiatives are cited and quantified	Economic rationale and overall execution Feasibility of initiative	Agreement to implement initiative from all relevant stakeholders	All actions completed	Savings tracked with measurable impact to bottom line
Details of savings initiative, required resources, and collaboration teams	Savings expectation supported by detailed data	Binding offer (RFP)	Final negotiations with supplier	Savings Savings clearly tracked and compliance confirmed
Quantitative estimate of required resources and impact to shareholders	Identification of market factors supporting savings expectation	Communication with key stakeholders regarding award of business	Paperwork uploaded and stored in appropriate systems	
Initial savings projection	Consultation with key stakeholders (e.g. Finance)			

Figure 21-2

Additionally, it is a good practice to focus on exceptions or trends. You can accomplish this by comparing your current P&L statement with past statements. Has anything changed drastically? If so, can you identify how or why?

Meet with a CPA, accountant, or financial analyst to get help identifying areas of improvement.

Continue to keep detailed records of your company's profits and losses so you can create new, accurate P&L statements every month or quarter.

Forecast your P&L to determine go-forward expected performance and measure accordingly.

PRO POINTERS

- P&L management is at the heart of every business. Knowing how to manage it well is a key to positive cash flow and overall success.

- Consider pushing financial responsibility down to the lowest management level. These team members are closest to the customer and can see what is required to serve them effectively and efficiently. Then tie incentives to both performance and profit.

- Properly managing P&L means properly managing and controlling key levers: pricing, payment terms, procurement, direct and variable costs, operating expenses and efficiency, supply chain optimization, customer growth, and an employee-centric culture.

- Use the cost-reduction methodology and don't overlook the fact that saving money positively impacts your P&L.

- Be sure to monitor trends and exceptions, comparing current P&L statements to previous ones and keeping detailed records.

- Use a professional to help you identify areas for improvement.

Chapter 22

RISK MANAGEMENT

"Risk is a function of how poorly a strategy
will perform if the 'wrong' scenario occurs."

—*Michael Porter*
Harvard Professor

Risk management is just as important P&L management since it is inherent in any business, and good risk management is essential to run a successful business. Risk cannot be eliminated, but it can be reduced and managed.

There are many types of business risk, some that can be controlled and others that cannot. What is important is how you anticipate risk and act to minimize it.

In this chapter, we will focus on a company's financial risks.

THE RISKS

There are four primary types of business risks: market risk, credit risk, liquidity risk, and operational risk.

Market risk encompasses the changing circumstances in an industry.

An example is the development of the sharing economy. Technology has enabled companies like Uber and Airbnb to thrive, while companies such as hotel and taxi companies that have been slow to adapt have suffered.

Companies need to focus on key business trends to ensure they are able to adapt to changes in the market and compete effectively on an ongoing basis. The most financially successful companies offer a unique value proposition that continues to evolve as the market changes.

Credit risk is the risk a company extends to customers who are provided products and/or services with the expectation the customer will pay for them at a later date.

Likewise, credit risk is also the amount of risk a supplier provides to your company. It is important to have credit so you can best manage the time gap between your receivables and payables.

A company must manage its credit obligations to have sufficient cash flow to pay its bills in a timely fashion. Otherwise, suppliers may reduce or stop extending credit, or refuse to be a supplier for your company.

Liquidity risk is the ability to access cash to meet financial obligations.

To manufacture products or offer services, companies make investments in assets, such as equipment, materials, or personnel. However, they need to balance these investments with daily operational needs. That is why liquidity risk includes both asset and operational funding liquidity risk. Asset liquidity is the company's ability to convert its assets into cash should there be a sudden, substantial need for additional cash flow. Operational funding liquidity is the ability to manage daily cash flow. Unexpected changes in revenue can present a substantial risk if the company doesn't have enough cash on hand to operate. This is why cash flow management is critical and why investors look at metrics such as free cash flow when evaluating companies.

Finally, *operational risks* are risks that can arise from a company's ordinary business activities. This includes, but isn't limited to, lawsuits, fraud risk, personnel problems, reputation, and business model risk.

A lawsuit can be distracting, diverting attention from day-to-day business operations.

Losing key personnel can also be disruptive since it requires focus to replace and retrain the right people and additional time for those people to get fully trained and be productive.

Business model issues can be challenging if your focus areas to grow your business are off target.

REAL-WORLD EXAMPLES

At USI and IEM, we took financial risks very seriously.

At IEM, we had an "asset light" model, meaning we didn't own or lease trucks or landfills. Instead, we invested in our people and technology, which were far less expensive and far more flexible and liquid.

We also had strong terms with our clients, as they were contractually required to pay for the service at the first of the month, a month in advance. We had strict penalties for those who paid late to best ensure on-time payment. For those late payers, we were like watch dogs in order to keep our accounts receivable at or less than 1 percent. Simply, we never took our eyes off this key part of our business.

Finally, we negotiated favorable terms with our suppliers. We typically paid in sixty to ninety days rather than fifteen to thirty days. Additionally, to keep our fixed investments in check, where possible, we bought used or refurbished equipment, as the difference between a new and refurbished compactor is very different than a new and old computer. A refurbished compactor worked as well at far less cost.

At USI, we were quite proud that we never, ever were involved in any litigation. This included clients, typically Fortune 500 companies, and suppliers, typically real estate brokers, landlords, construction companies, architects, and technology companies, among others.

Our approach was to do everything we could to do an exceptional job and do things the right way on every project. When something went inadvertently wrong, we took accountability for our error and made things right. If we believed we were falsely accused, we proactively addressed this situation with the other party and avoided a prolonged dispute. This also protected our reputational risk in that we were viewed as a company who put our clients first.

The Continuous Improvement Process we took at both USI and IEM that I would recommend for you is shown in Figure 22-1, the Continuous Improvement Process.

Continuous Improvement Process

Figure 22-1

A description of this process is:

1. Identify the risks

   Uncover, recognize, and assess the risks that might affect your company or its outcomes.

2. Analyze consequences

   Determine the probability and impact of each risk. Companies need to develop an understanding of the nature of the risk and its potential to affect project goals and objectives.

3. Evaluate potential impact

   Evaluate and rank the risk according to its potential impact, which should be determined by combining the potential likelihood and the consequence. A decision then needs to be made about whether the risk is acceptable or whether it is serious enough to warrant treatment.

4. Address the issues

   Create a plan to treat the highest-ranked risks to achieve acceptable risk levels with the following risk-management solutions:

   - *Avoidance* – Eliminate the risk in its entirety. For example, if you have some high-performing employees you want to remain on your team, invest in more compensation, training, or meaningful assignments for these teams.
   - *Mitigation* – Reduce the risk. For example, for a manufacturing company that relies on 24/7 uptime to keep creating products, any downtime can be truly detrimental. As a result, implementing a preventative maintenance plan and

having an inventory of spare parts can help reduce this risk.

- *Transfer* – Transfer the threat by outsourcing the risk to a third party, such as a supplier who can house materials or an insurance company to assist in the incident of loss as a result of the risk.
- *Incur* – Accept the risk and budget accordingly. For example, if the cost is manageable and acting quickly is prudent, this may be a way to "make it go away."

5. Monitor and review

All risks should be regularly monitored, tracked, and reviewed by a team of employees, and implementation should be driven from the executive and board level to team leaders, managers, and staff. When properly addressed, risks can be removed from the list. When a risk isn't fully mitigated, the solutions need to be reviewed. When a new risk arises, the process needs to start over.

PRO POINTERS

- Risk cannot be eliminated, but it can be mitigated and managed.

- The four main financial risks to a business include market risk, credit risk, liquidity risk, and operational risk.

- To avoid credit risk (both in terms of receivables and payables), keep a close eye on late-paying customers and put contractual, strict penalties in place for late payment. On the flip side, negotiate the most favorable terms possible with vendors and suppliers.

- Doing an exceptional job and doing things the right way on every project is key to minimizing risk.

- When things go wrong, be accountable and address issues proactively.

- The five-step process to managing risk: identify risks, analyze consequences, evaluate potential impact, employ a management solution (avoidance, mitigation, transfer, incur), and monitor and review.

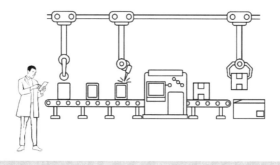

OPERATE EFFICIENTLY

Chapter 23

IDENTIFY AND PRIORITIZE PROCESSES

"I have two kinds of problems, the urgent and
the important. The urgent are not important,
and the important are never urgent."

—*Dwight D. Eisenhower*
Army General and US President

Imagine you get a coupon in your mail offering a discount to bring your car to a new local oil change service provider, Discount Oil Change. You bring your car in and wait patiently for the work to be completed. Half an hour or so later, you drive off, pleased you invested in maintaining your vehicle, saving a couple of dollars in the process.

As you leave the lot, you notice that something doesn't feel right. So, you pull over and notice a trail of oil and a deflated tire. You turn around and drive back to Discount Oil Change, wondering what happened.

The service manager apologizes for the oversight and tries to address the issues promptly, then offers you a credit for the next oil change, but the damage has already been done. The company has lost you as a customer.

Conversely, McDonald's has been such a strong company for so many years. Why? From its inception, it has embraced a process focusing on speed and consistency. Its food isn't the highest quality—we're not talking gourmet food here—but you know what to expect anywhere and anytime, and that is comforting.

In conducting business, companies perform a variety of activities to make products, deliver services, sell new business, collaborate with team members, manage finances, and numerous others. As a result, the lesson here is to maintain quality execution, companies need to have a playbook or checklist for all activities, especially ones that are customer facing. Don't be like Discount Oil Change.

As soon as you start managing an initiative, department, or company and need to entrust others to do productive work, it is critical to have processes outlined and training developed. This way, there is a protocol or playbook to follow for consistent execution. Consistent execution is what has allowed McDonald's to succeed and grow globally.

My suggestion is that you lock yourself and your leadership team in a room and identify all major activities that the business undertakes. By major, I mean those that are important, visible, and can impact the top and/or bottom line.

Before you go any further, note most leaders don't prioritize these requirements soon enough or at all because the day-to-day requirements of managing the business pull at them. The emails keep coming and the phone keeps ringing. Don't go there. Your investment now in developing processes will make your life easier downstream, I promise.

Processes can generally be categorized by function, as you can see in Figure 23-1, Process Categories.

Process Categories

Function	Sub-Function
Leadership	Team Management
	Customer Relations
	Innovation
Sales	Business Development
	Product Development
Marketing	Market Research
	Lead Generation
	Marketing/Sales Materials
	CRM Database
	Website
Human Resources	Hiring
	Staff Training/Development
	Job Descriptions
Finance	Budgeting
	Forecasting
	P&L Management
	Accounts Receivable
Operations	Account Management
	Product Delivery
	Leveraging Technology
	Workflow

Figure 23-1

USING POST-ITS

One of the best ways to use the tools I present in this chapter is to get in a room and, using Post-it notes (that can easily be rearranged . . . and removed), determine each task that is done now in any given process, the steps required, and the responsible team member. It may seem archaic, but, as shown in the below figure, it is a very effective way to map your as-is state.

With a wall full of Post-its, you can easily begin to see the complexity of the process you're mapping and may quickly start to discern steps that are cumbersome or, in fact, are completely unnecessary. To operate most efficiently, every process must be pared down to only the necessary tasks. You'll have an easier time streamlining tasks once you see the entire process picture, and you'll be better able to determine the gap between where you are and where you want to be in terms of greater efficiency.

Post-it Notes Whiteboard

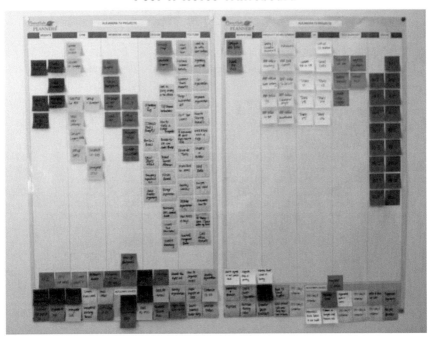

Figure 23-2

DEFINING PROCESSES

The mapping of the as-is (or current state) process can be divided into two phases. First is a high-level view or Discovery Diagram, then we can get more detailed with a specific Process Diagram.

Creating a Discovery Diagram gets the juices flowing. It is a high-level map that is usually six to ten phases long. It usually contains just these phases without any decision points or diamonds, as you'll see in the Process Diagram.

An example from the above list under Human Resources is the hiring process. See Figure 23-3 below.

Discovery Diagram

Create Position → Post Position → Screen Candidates → Interview Candidates → Make Offer → Offer Accepted/Rejected

Figure 23-3

You may ask, "What if I can't create a Discovery Diagram because each task is fairly unique?" For those very unique tasks, you shouldn't be creating a process, but for those activities listed in Figure 23-3, you should have one. These are common to almost all businesses. If there are specific attributes that are different, you can flag them, document them, and manage accordingly.

Once the Discovery Diagram is completed, you can create a Process Diagram. Here, high-level processes are broken into more detailed processes, also called "swim lanes." These include roles and responsibilities as well as activities.

Process Diagram

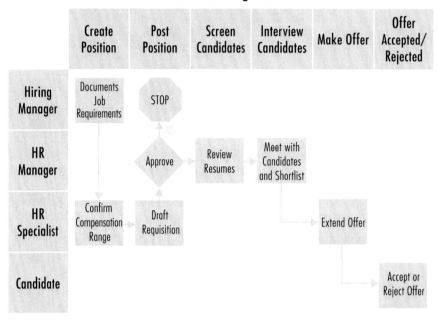

Figure 23-4

Once you've mapped out your processes, you should have a better idea how things are managed and can assess which detailed processes are most critical to the business and which are repeatable. If you identify processes that fulfill both characteristics, you have a strong opportunity to drive consistent value. From the game Scrabble, I call this a "Double Word Score."

First, to determine what is most critical to address, I use the following matrix as seen in Figure 23-5.

The columns highlight key criteria to consider, weigh, and score for each process. They include:

- Broken Process: A broken process is one that hampers productivity, given it hasn't been executed consistently.
- Constraint: This is an area to check if the process is a critical path item or one that will cause bottlenecks if not executed properly.
- Growth Contributor: This focuses on a financial payoff. This can pertain to sales, customer care, and/or product quality.
- Cause of Frustration: This is an area in your company that creates challenges to effectively deliver a product or service and hampers team productivity as a result.
- Easy to Implement: The final category highlights processes that are easiest and fastest to implement.

An example of a completed Process Prioritization Matrix is seen in Figure 23-6. Based on the results, the highlighted processes, which scored highest, are the ones to focus on first.

Process Prioritization Matrix

Function	Sub-Function
Leadership	Team Management
	Customer Relations
	Innovation
Sales	Business Development
	Product Development
Marketing	Market Research
	Lead Generation
	Marketing/Sales Materials
	CRM Database
	Website
Human Resources	Hiring
	Staff Training/Development
	Job Descriptions
Finance	Budgeting
	Forecasting
	P&L Management
	Accounts Receivable
Operations	Account Management
	Product Delivery
	Leveraging Technology
	Workflow

Broken Process	Constraint	Growth Contributor	Cause of Frustration	Easy to Implement	Score
3 points	3 points	2 points	1 point	1 point	

Figure 23-5

Process Prioritization Scoring Table

Function	Sub-Function
Leadership	Team Management
	Customer Relations
	Innovation
Sales	Business Development
	Product Development
Marketing	Market Research
	Lead Generation
	Marketing/Sales Materials
	CRM Database
	Website
Human Resources	Hiring
	Staff Training/Development
	Job Descriptions
Finance	Budgeting
	Forecasting
	P&L Management
	Accounts Receivable
Operations	Account Management
	Product Delivery
	Leveraging Technology
	Workflow

Broken Process 3 points	Constraint 3 points	Growth Contributor 2 points	Cause of Frustration 1 point	Easy to Implement 1 point	Score
✓	✓	✓	✓		9
✓		✓			5
✓	✓	✓			8
✓	✓	✓			8
		✓			2
				✓	1
✓					3
✓				✓	4
					0
				✓	1
✓	✓	✓			8
✓					3
				✓	1
✓				✓	4
✓					3
✓	✓	✓			8
✓	✓				6
✓	✓				6
				✓	1
✓					3
✓	✓	✓			8

Figure 23-6

PRO POINTERS

- Without documented processes for your business, you will struggle with consistent delivery of your product or service. Without consistent delivery, sustained growth is impossible. Think McDonald's.

- When you entrust others to do productive work, it is critical to have processes outlined and training developed.

- Despite unceasing emails and ringing phones, you must take time to identify and prioritize all major activities. It will pay off.

- Using Post-its on a wall is a very effective way to map out your current state.

- Start with a Discovery Diagram that is a high-level overview of the activity.

- Next, develop a Process Diagram that more specifically identifies who does what and the flow of the activity through your organization.

- Finally, use the Process Prioritization Matrix to determine which activities require process documentation first.

Chapter 24

STANDARDIZE AND DETERMINE AUTOMATION OPPORTUNITIES

"I fear not the man who has practiced ten
thousand kicks once, but I fear the man who
has practiced one kick ten thousand times."

— *Bruce Lee*
Martial Artist

As you've read, each chapter of this book starts with a relevant and inspirational quote. I happen to really like this chapter's quote, because it transcends business and life. Simply, if you focus on one thing and do it consistently well, you will succeed.

Given that you now have prioritized your processes, you will need to focus on these processes and determine which ones are repeatable so you can do fewer things consistently well.

As with the McDonald's example, having consistent quality execution is key, but it also drives efficiency that contributes to the bottom line.

Before McDonald's created a consistent, repeatable process for fast food, Henry Ford changed the auto and manufacturing industries. He wanted to make automobiles more affordable for the greater population, so he created a system of mass production that created a consistent, quality product at reduced costs.

From a manufacturing perspective, Ford created standard execution or work for repeatable tasks. This was demonstrated on the assembly line but still focused on human-led work. Today, many of these processes are partially or fully automated, creating even greater efficiency.

What did McDonald's and Ford have in common? They standardized and industrialized their most important processes that delivered value to customers.

Applying this to your company, you should think the same way. If a process is manual and inconsistent and you are executing it poorly with ten staff and a hundred customers, how is it going to work with a hundred staff and one thousand customers? The answer is it won't.

> **Automating processes that are a regular part of your business is key to your success. McDonald's and Ford understood the importance of standardized processes.**

Based on the list of processes you have prioritized, determine which ones can and should be executed in the same manner each and every single time. The hiring process is a natural for standardization. So is managing a pipeline.

REAL-WORLD EXAMPLES

At USI, we managed portfolios of properties for our corporate clients. We realized real estate was a transactional business and most companies hired brokers and managed projects on a one-off basis. Although this could be effective, it rarely drove efficiency.

Larger or more complex projects drew an inordinate amount of attention, where smaller ones were often left for local teams to pick up the pieces.

We drove value by standardizing the process to drive efficiency. In doing so, we could handle more activity and portfolio churn with fewer resources. We were, therefore, able to win business and add great value on nationally distributed portfolios, starting with national staffing companies, including Adecco, Manpower, and Randstad. They had several hundred locations, but the average location was two thousand square feet, which is pretty small.

At IEM, we created efficiency managing the waste stream for retail property owners and their tenants. Previously, each property was managed individually and locally. Property managers would tour the compactor locations and determine when they were nearly full, at which time they would call the disposal company to pick up the trash. We created a system to best understand the cycle of trash pickups based on location, property type, and tenant mix. By doing so, we not only were more efficient but also more effective, as the fewer times the disposal company came, the less expensive it was for the customers.

One of the most effective ways to ensure consistency in business processes is to automate them, increasing throughput while eliminating most of the human errors that can affect the scaling of operations.

At USI, we automated by creating a proprietary system that we used to serve our clients and charged for it accordingly. The online software was called Sequentra, which stood for sequential tracking. Using this system, we had a central administration function to manage all client real estate–related information, including locations, rent, operating expenses, and even asset tracking. With this, we'd generate reports or queries that enabled us to act on the most timely or important requirements. At the same time, the system incorporated a complementary project management module, so any activity that resulted from the administration function could be automated and managed consistently.

Using Sequentra, we were able to manage 30 percent or more

activity and do so far more confidently. Clients were thrilled, as they paid less and got more. One client suggested that the direct feed from Sequentra to their accounts payable system reduced their manual rent payment process by 90 percent.

At IEM, we developed a sensor-based system called Waste Management Control System (WMCS). We placed sensors in the compactors that gave us real-time pressure readings. When the compactor was nearly full and ready to be emptied or pulled, the sensor reading reached a pounds-per-square inch or PSI level. This was far more effective than the prior manual process, in which we took a well-informed but somewhat educated guess.

Using WMCS, we were able to increase resource capacity by 20 percent and reduce costs by 25 percent. That created another $2 million in annual net profit, which was pretty significant.

At my current company, Midcourse Advisors, we provide consulting services, typically on a project basis. As such, we need a consistent way to launch and manage a project. The sequential steps we use that incorporate automation include the following, as itemized in Figure 24-1:

Project Automation

CREATE CLIENT FOLDER	Create client/project folder on Google Drive. Add client agreement and other relevant documentation.
ANNOUNCE PROJECT	Announce project with internal email to team.
SET UP FINANCIALS	Set up client in company financial system.
SET UP TEAMWORK	Create new project using teamwork project management application.
IMPORT PROJECT TEMPLATES	Import project templates based on project type.
KICK OFF PROJECT	Team meeting to kick off project.
EXECUTE PROJECT	Complete project.

Figure 24-1

I believe that compound interest is to your money as automation is to your time, so getting projects set up well and automated is paramount to success.

There are numerous software solutions available to help you achieve automation. Your choice depends on your industry, infrastructure, and budget. As the alternatives are enhanced and continually change, for a list of automated software solutions, please visit www.midcourseadvisors.com/growlikeapro.

Just as important as investing in new software is, make sure your infrastructure to support use of it is up to date and able to scale. As you scale operations, you will be bringing in extra staff and hopefully attracting many more customers, so you need to ensure your processes cover the regular monitoring and upgrading of the infrastructure that services these areas. If you don't have sufficient storage for Google Drive, licenses for your automation solution, or alignment for consistent team execution, all your effort may be wasted.

When you are ready to scale operations, you need to consider many factors, but chief among these should be how to keep consistent business processes to ensure the scaling is smooth and seamless for both staff and customers.

PRO POINTERS

- Focus on one task repeated numerous times rather than numerous tasks only repeated once.

- Determine standard execution or work for repeatable tasks to gain efficiency and profitability.

- Standardization is not limited to manufacturing— either cars or burgers. Every business can standardize many of its activities.

- With today's ever-changing technology, there is always a way to automate.

- Ensure that your infrastructure will accommodate your automation and be able to scale with growth.

Chapter 25

ALIGN RESOURCES

"Get the right people in the right seats on the bus."

—*Jim Collins*
Author of Good to Great

You've created processes and automated them where possible.

You've assigned positions to manage the systems.

As we've discussed, there's a methodology to hiring or engaging with your staff in order to continue to inspire and develop them. You need to make sure that the staffers have clarity on their responsibilities in order to execute.

To start, you have to understand your role and the best use of your time and skill set. Leaders should be the ones predicting the future and creating vision and strategy to achieve that vision. Then leaders delegate and leverage others to move the business in the right direction.

Michael Coles (co-founder of Great American Cookies and former CEO of Caribou Coffee) understands leadership. He has been a good mentor and friend. Of the many sage pieces of advice he has shared with me, the one that has resonated the most is that leaders can't possibly do and know everything. What is most important is to know enough about each company function so you can ask the right questions. If you understand this concept and can apply it well, you will be able to identify the key opportunities to pursue, the key challenges to address, and the key personnel to manage them.

To achieve this, I've created the Business Offense System in Figure 25-1 that focuses on those two key tenets for leadership: predicting the future and leveraging others.

Business Offense System

Figure 25-1

In the United States, there are more than six million registered companies. Given the lower market barriers to entry, more than five hundred thousand companies with employees are started each year. With all of these companies hitting the market, why are only 4 percent achieving annual revenues of $1 million annually, and why can only 1 percent sustain it for more than two years?

The reason is that business founders who have started new companies often feel challenged once their business grows beyond eight employees or contractors. At that point, the company has grown sufficiently to require dedicated functions other than fundraising, product/service development, and sales. These include marketing, finance, operations, technology applications, and human resources, among others.

Many business founders struggle with this growth milestone, as they are accustomed to knowing everything going on day to day in the business and managing everything closely. It's understandable, as this is what is required to launch, maintain liquidity, and sustain the business. But managing this way creates a ceiling, limiting growth and the ability to scale.

Jeff Bradford, president and CEO of the Bradford Group, a public relations firm, saw his company grow 47 percent once he got out of the way. He says, "Starting a business requires a high tolerance for risk, comfort with change, a ruthless focus on results, lots of energy, high expectations of everyone around you, and the ability to ignore naysayers. Some of these skills and attitudes—like ruthlessness and ignoring naysayers—are counterproductive to running versus starting a business. Noticeably absent from this list are 'people skills.'"[14]

Similarly, I recently worked with a client who encountered similar challenges. He simply didn't trust others to do what he could do far better. When I reviewed with him what he did best and what he could achieve by focusing on that and letting others do the rest, he relented. We hired a junior team, trained them, and let them go do the needed, but less-mission-critical, work. Since then, his business has doubled.

Using the Business Offense System enables small business leaders to overcome this major challenge.

BUSINESS OFFENSE SYSTEM

The first tenet, predicting the future, includes two major components: vision and strategy.

A company's vision is what it wants to achieve and when. Without a defined path, companies tend to move ahead somewhat without direction, inhibiting the likelihood of success. In fact, one of my favorite quotes on this topic is from Lewis Carroll, the author of *Alice's Adventures in Wonderland*: "If you don't know where you're going, any road will get you there."

---

14 Jeff Bradford, "Three Strategies That Helped Us Become a Growth Company," *Forbes*, November 5, 2018, https://www.forbes.com/sites/forbesagencycouncil/2018/11/05/three-strategies-that-helped-us-become-a-growth-company/#6ceda3a3454d.

As a result, having a vision is essential, and the more specific the vision is, the better.

For example, Big Nerd Ranch wanted to expand its penetration into the Fortune 500 realm. We defined its vision as, "We will build relationships that drive partnerships with twenty Fortune 500 companies by 2020."

By being specific about what the company wanted to achieve and when, it had a well-defined tool to run the business. In fact, it became a filter to ensure everyone on the team was aligned and moving to achieve the vision.

When hiring, management asked, "Will these roles and the individuals we hire help us achieve our vision?"

When management pursued client opportunities, they asked, "Will these potential clients help us achieve our vision?"

When they hosted meetings, they asked, "Is the agenda focused on activities that will help us achieve our vision?"

If the answer to any of these pursuits was no, the pursuits were abandoned, saving time and money to focus on the most impactful activities.

While a vision is important and sets the tone for the company's work, it doesn't define how the company will get there. That's where strategy comes into play. To successfully scale, a company needs a robust strategy. It is one that matters enough to customers and differentiates it from the competition.

Prior to setting a strategy, I pay particular attention to trends. I want to know what opportunities may exist, what my competition is doing, and what I should avoid pursuing. Currently, there are three mega-trends that are or will affect every business. These include technology, demographics, and regulation.

Demographics are dominated by baby boomers and millennials. More than eighty million baby boomers are entering the latter stages of their careers and are now starting to retire. This rat making its way through the snake creates opportunities for financial services firms, healthcare providers, senior living developers, etc. At the same time, more than eighty-four million millennials have entered or will be entering the work force. These young professionals represent more than one-third of current workers, which will increase rapidly to more than two-thirds by 2025. Opportunities exist for companies that offer environmentally friendly products and provide flexibility and meaning for their employees. Millennials tend to live and work close to the cities, providing jobs for real estate owners, retailers, and those who take advantage of the on-demand community (Uber, Airbnb, etc.).

The rapid ongoing change in technology enables companies to execute and deliver faster and cheaper than ever before. Companies that are engaged in data analysis, machine learning, artificial intelligence, and IoT (sensors/internet of things applications) are expanding the fastest, employing the most people, and occupying the most office space. At the time of this writing, in Atlanta, 40 percent of the absorption in office space is being driven by expanding technology companies.

Finally, there will need to be ongoing regulation. What parameters will exist for self-driving cars? How will sensors be used for public advantage/disadvantage? Will our privacy be more or less protected though social media platforms where access to information is readily available for us as well as about us? How will tax laws continue to change?

Once you have identified these trends, you need to create a strategy that acknowledges them and focuses on your strengths to exploit them while avoiding those where you may be weak.

A strategy model I use is based on a Balanced Scorecard methodology. It is geared to help you focus on the tasks that best help you achieve your company's vision. The high-level model with example goals and measurements is seen in Figure 25-2, Goals and Measurements.

Goals and Measurements

Vision	%	Goals	Measurements
Finance & Stakeholders	35%	Reduce overhead by 10%	Reduced cost
Customers & Markets	25%	Increase market share by 15%	Incremental market share
Operations & Production	25%	Produce 50 more "widgets" per day	Production results
Learning & Innovation	15%	Develop 2 VPs to oversee new product offerings	Promotion, training, and turnover of P&Ls

Figure 25-2

ASSIGNMENT	Time to pause and put what you learned to work. Identify all tasks you and your team can delegate and thoughtfully transition the work.

Once a vision and strategy have been developed, you need to be able to leverage others to complete the work successfully. It starts with operations.

The opportunity to grow and scale can only be achieved through operational efficiency and consistency. This is critical, as repeatable tasks should be executed in the same manner each and every time. By doing so, you will have better confidence in outcomes, making it even easier to delegate. And you won't have to hire as many people as you will be able to get work done better and faster. I really embrace this, as it enables workers to use creativity to face customers more directly and solve more challenging problems on their behalf. This, in turn, creates more impact and value for both employees and customers.

The operational excellence model is demonstrated in Figure 25-3.

Operational Excellence Model

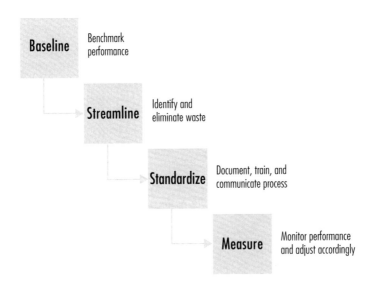

Figure 25-3

Key trends in this area include transparency, where tools such as Slack and others are available for greater openness, accountability, and collaboration. These are all good things.

Tying strategy to operations is accomplished as seen in Figure 25-4.

Strategic Action Plan

Vision	Goals	Applicable Trends	Actions
Finance & Stakeholders	Reduce overhead by 10%	Regulation	Lobby to reduce compliance requirements
Customers & Markets	Increase market share by 15%	Demographics	Target millennials who live in top 10 cities
Operations & Production	Produce 50 more "widgets" per day	Technology	Employ new production system
Learning & Innovation	Develop 2 VPs to oversee new product offerings	Demographics	Develop mentor/ training program

Figure 25-4

The last step to achieve scale is to delegate. My view is delegation is about getting the right butts in the right seats doing the right work.

Simply, when you seek to delegate, you need to assess the functions and tasks that are being performed. That is what we would accomplish in the standardize step of the operational excellence model.

Once you have such a list detailed, you should determine what activities are most urgent and important that only you have the unique skill set to tackle. As Figure 25-5 indicates, almost any other activity can and should be delegated.

Activity Prioritization

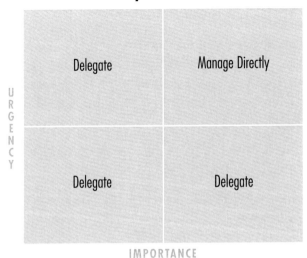

Figure 25-5

For example, key customer relationship opportunities or challenges may fall into the Manage Directly category. Developing and supporting the company vision and overseeing the strategic plan may also fall into Manage Directly. Managing daily operations or finances may be tasks that should be delegated, as they are important but aren't as urgent.

Once these tasks have been identified and categorized, the delegated tasks need to be assigned. They should be assigned to those who have the skill, will, and capacity to do so. Without commitment from the assignee, it doesn't matter what authority the assignor has. Then, they need to be given the support (resources/tools) to succeed. Ongoing measurement and check-in will allow for feedback and adjustment as required.

RACI MATRIX

The tool I recommend using to connect the right resources to the right positions (a.k.a. right butts in the right seats) is called a RACI Matrix. RACI stands for Responsible, Accountable, Consulted, and Informed, corresponding to four association types, detailed as follows:

1. **Responsible:** Those in this role complete the tasks required. For example, a marketing manager may be responsible for writing and posting blogs.

2. **Accountable:** Those in this role are accountable for the deliverable or outcome of a task. In other words, they have authority and the "buck stops with them." Using the same example, this person is accountable that the writing and posting are completed in a quality and timely manner but doesn't actually do the work.

3. **Consulted:** A role that is consulted is an advisor to a task. For example, a social media guru may be consulted as a subject matter expert. Note: Advisors should be considered carefully, as too many people in this role can elongate task time and increase the risk of poor performance.

4. **Informed:** A role that is informed is updated on task completion. For example, a sales executive may require status updates on an upgrade being completed on the software they sell.

The RACI Matrix provides the following benefits:

- Provides role clarity
- Ensures proper allocation of resources
- Establishes tasks aren't overlooked
- Enables resource reallocation when the team has turnover

RACI Matrix

		Role											
		Project Leadership			Project Team Members			Project Sub-Teams			External Resources		
		Position	Position	Position	Position	Position	Position	Position	Position	Position	Position	Position	Position
Project Deliverable (or Activity)	Task												
	Task												
	Task												
	Task												
	Task												
R					Responsible								
A					Accountable								
C					Consulted								
I					Informed								

Figure 25-6

For your reference, a completed RACI Matrix for a strategic savings project is shown in Figure 25-7.

Completed RACI Matrix

		Role								
		Project Leadership				Project Team Members				Project Sub-Teams
Project Deliverable (or Activity)		CEO	CFO	COO	VP Sourcing	Real Estate Mgr	Freight Mgr	Mfg Mgr	Travel Mgr	Professional Svcs Mgr	Financial Mgr
	Identify Savings	I	C	C	A	R	R	R	R	R	C
	Evaluate Savings	I	C	C	A	R	R	R	R	R	C
	Confirm Savings	I	C	C	A	R	R	R	R	R	C
	Negotiate Savings	I	C	C	A	R	R	R	R	R	C
	Realize Savings	I	C	C	A	R	R	R	R	R	C
R						Responsible				
A						Accountable				
C						Consulted				
I						Informed				

Figure 25-7

PRO POINTERS

- Staff members must first have clarity about their responsibilities in order to properly execute in their position.

- As the leader, your job is to predict the future, using the Business Offense System, and then leverage others.

- Predicting the future relies on vision and strategy. Leveraging others includes operational efficiency and delegation.

- A RACI Matrix is the ideal tool for connecting the right resources with the right positions.
    - R: Responsible – Completes required tasks.
    - A: Accountable – The buck stops here and those in this role are accountable for the outcome, typically for an on-time and quality delivery.
    - C: Consulted – Serves in an advisory capacity.
    - I: Informed – Is updated on progress. Often, top management positions fall here, but it can also incorporate other levels.

Chapter 26

ENVISION GROWTH

"Imagination is not only the uniquely human capacity to envision that which is not, and therefore the fount of all invention and innovation."

—*J. K. Rowling*
Author

Over my career, on occasion, I have worked with a number of accomplished leaders who inadvertently fall into the trap of what I call "The Cycle of Good Enough." This occurs when business is going well and leaders don't stay on their *A Game*. When complacency sets in and things are going well, it may not be an issue. But when things don't go well, this can be dangerous to a business.

The Cycle of Good Enough typically occurs when:

1. You have had some success with your business and you don't keep pushing yourself and your teams to do more or better.

OR

2. You hit a road bump that can derail your business and you choose to "make do" or ignore it altogether.

Two quotes sum up what a false sense of security can do to negatively impact your business. I would claim neither is envisioning growth.

The first is, "Neither RedBox nor Netflix are even on the radar screen in terms of competition." This was stated by the CEO of Blockbuster, Jim Keyes.[15]

The other is, "The Apple Watch is an interesting toy, but not a revolution."[16]

What business leaders need to realize is how fast their businesses can be disrupted. It used to be quite a process to start and grow a business because of the speed and cost of resources. Nowadays, virtually anyone can:

- Incorporate online for a few hundred dollars
- Raise money from crowdsourcing sites such as Kickstarter
- Hire programmers from Upwork
- Rent computer-processing power from Amazon
- Find manufacturers on Alibaba
- Arrange payments via Square
- Immediately set about conquering the world

Successful business leaders are strong managers of risk. They spend each day running their businesses, but the best thing they can do is reduce their risk profiles.

The best business leaders are always thinking a step ahead and challenging their organizations to achieve more.

Take, for example, Brian Chesky, the co-founder of Airbnb. He started the company in 2008 when he couldn't find a room in Washington, DC, at President Obama's inauguration.

He found a real need, then initially developed a rudimentary

15 Rick Munarriz, "Blockbuster CEO Has Answers: An Interview with Kim Keyes Shows His Confidence," *The Motley Fool*, April 5, 2017, https://www.fool.com/investing/general/2008/12/10/blockbuster-ceo-has-answers.aspx.

16 Samuel Gibbs, "Swatch CEO: Apple Watch Is 'Interesting Toy' That Can't Last More Than 24 Hours," *The Guardian*, August 24, 2015, https://www.theguardian.com/technology/2015/aug/24/swatch-ceo-apple-watch-interesting-toy.

platform and signed up some initial customers who wanted to rent out a part of or all their properties. The number of customers plateaued quickly, so he took action and sought direct feedback by offering free photography to potential property listers. The valuable feedback he secured was that they wanted to have a profile of potential customers so they felt safe to rent. Chesky listened and built profile requirement, after which the business grew drastically.

But Chesky didn't stop there. He wasn't complacent. He wanted the organization to think differently and envision growth.

To accomplish this and improve, differentiate, even disrupt, they decided *to think of what is possible.* The following chart demonstrates how this works.

AirBnB View of What Is Possible

Level 1	Level 3	Level 5	Level 7	Level 9	Level 10
Rent a room	Rent a room	Rent a room	Rent a room	Rent a room	Rent a room
	Greeting	Greeting	Greeting	Greeting	Greeting
	Gift basket	Gift basket	Gift basket	Gift basket	Gift basket
		Surfboard	Surfboard	Surfboard	Surfboard
			Loaned car	Loaned car	Loaned car
			Restaurant reservation	Restaurant reservation	Restaurant reservation
				Picked up at airport	Picked up at airport
					Elon Musk

Figure 26-1

Chesky gathered his leadership team and challenged them to think about what Airbnb could offer to provide more value to its customers and therefore grow more and make more money.

The framework starts from the left, where Chesky suggested

they had a good business, but it was a Level 1. It was an available room that wasn't in a hotel setting at a competitive price.

They then brainstormed what more they could do, regardless of time, finances, or other constraints.

They determined that a Level 3 would be more valuable if hosts not only rented properties, but also greeted customers when they arrived and provided a gift basket.

They upped their game at Level 5, where a beachfront property that catered to surfers actually had a surfboard that could be used.

Level 7 added providing the use of a car and making an exclusive restaurant reservation.

The stakes keep increasing to Level 10, where Elon Musk picks you up at the airport and then flies with you to Mars. That's right—to Mars!

Once all the ideas were flushed out to determine what was possible, reaching up to Level 10, Chesky facilitated having the team evaluate what was feasible.

Was traveling to Mars with Elon Musk feasible? Of course not.

But Level 7 was. In fact, they created a concierge service, including two offerings. They are now the fastest-growing segments in the Airbnb business.

The first is called Experiences, like going truffle hunting or driving classic cars, which are led by locals. Airbnb brokers the payment from the user to the guide and takes a cut, similar to how its home-booking service works. The other is called Places, which are recommendations from local residents. Airbnb has some revenue-sharing deals in place, like a partnership with Resy to book restaurant reservations.

If you want to think different, as with Airbnb, you need to focus on what is possible for your business. In order to do this, you need to be in the right frame of mind to think a bit "out of the box."

So how do you envision what is possible?

Envisioning is:

- Knowing what you and your company are good at doing currently and what makes you unique
- Understanding what you've tried to do before to grow your business and what worked and didn't work
- Building on your knowledge and understanding to further explore what opportunities can further differentiate you and your team

Think what you could do if you didn't have any constraints on your business, including time and money. What would you do to grow your business?

Using this methodology, I coached a training company to expand its offerings from in-class trainings to provide enhanced offerings. The first incorporated online learning for customers who didn't want to take as much time and expense to travel to the training. The second was a more highly customized experience for those who did travel, including specific engagement, learning, and certification that could only be achieved in person.

ASSIGNMENT

Time to pause and put what you learned to work.

Gather your leadership team and determine what is possible, and what is then feasible for your business.

PRO POINTERS

- Complacent leaders leave their businesses open to be disrupted.

- One way to overcome this is to work with your teams to envision growth and explore what is possible.

- Then you can determine what is feasible and plan to implement it.

- Be the disrupter, not the disrupted.

Chapter 27

CREATE SHORT BURSTS OF FOCUSED EFFORT

"You don't get results by focusing on results. You get results by focusing on the actions that produce results."

—*Mike Hawkins*
Actor

In 2019, Eliud Kipchoge made history by becoming the first person to run a marathon distance in under two hours. The thirty-four-year-old Kenyan long-distance runner completed 26.2 miles in 1 hour 59 minutes 40 seconds at the Ineos 1:59 Challenge in Vienna, Austria.

Kipchoge did not achieve this feat by solely running marathons.

In fact, to stoke speed, he not only ran near race pace over distances of four hundred meters or more, but also got even faster with super-short, super-fast efforts, sometimes referred to as high-intensity interval training (HIIT).

Not unlike Kipchoge, running and growing a business may

be more of a marathon, but the adjustments that can be made along the journey should include some short bursts of focused effort.

Without focus, near-term initiatives cannot be accomplished. I recommend you make a list of what you need to accomplish in the next ninety days by focusing on the following:

1. Commitments to Uphold

   Unless this is the first day in your business, you have existing commitments to uphold. For example, this can be products or services contracted to deliver. You need to acknowledge these commitments as you focus on other business priorities.

2. Decisions to Make

   To move a business forward and grow, you have some key decisions to make on an ongoing basis. Placing some time-bound parameters forces you to acquire the needed information to make a decision, good or bad, and move on.

3. Things to Stop Doing

   Just as important as making decisions on potentially new activities, it is important to dismiss areas of effort that are unproductive or won't get you where you want to go.

4. Relationships to Cultivate

   Growing a business revolves around meeting new people who either have the pain point you have identified and can solve or those who know or can influence those who do. You always need to be cultivating such relationships.

5. Opportunities to Pursue

   Specific opportunities should continue to be

identified and sought. These may be new customers, new partnerships, new products or services, etc.

For a downloadable copy of a 90-Day Focus Worksheet, go to www.midcourseadvisors.com/growlikeapro.

ADD URGENCY

In addition to focus, you need to have urgency. Even if you are focused, unless you feel the pressure to complete the tasks at hand in a quality manner as quickly as possible, you can focus aimlessly for quite some time.

You can do the following three things to create a sense of urgency:

1. Let customer expectations drive the urgency.

    Determine the highest priorities to fulfill in order to exceed customer expectations. Communicate this to team members and what the benefit of doing so will do for the business and themselves. Employees will do what it takes to fulfill the company promise.

2. Set daily, weekly, and monthly goals.

    Speed and urgency naturally increase as people get closer to a deadline. For example, employee productivity accelerates to meet a shipping or project milestone goal by the end of the week. It is a good idea to post results and hold people accountable for achieving the stated goal.

3. Create financial or other incentives.

    Self-interest is highly motivating for most people. A good incentive system—financial or otherwise—will lift employees, speed processes, and drive down unit costs.

PRO POINTERS

- Running a business is a marathon, but to excel and grow, you have to practice sprints as well.

- Keep a list of near-term initiatives to accomplish in the next ninety days, including commitments to uphold, needed decisions, activities to cease doing, relationships to cultivate, and opportunities to pursue.

- Always add urgency to keep things moving forward and growing.

TRACK PERFORMANCE

Chapter 28

MEASURE AND ADJUST

"If you can't measure every part of your business, you can't manage or grow it."

—Peter Drucker
Business Management Guru and Author

Creating a system that leverages processes and automation is a great effort that results in opportunities to scale your business well. As I mentioned, investing the time and effort to identify and document processes always pays off. However, it doesn't stop there.

Success and scalable growth lie in predictable execution—it's the link between ideas and reality. The building blocks of predictable execution include:

- Shared mission, vision, and values.
- Unity behind a powerful mission and vision from every member of the organization from the C-suite to the shipping door. Established quarterly strategic objectives.
- Clarity on goals and tasks, with measurable targets, and how they roll up into the mission. There should

be no more than five to seven organizational objectives that are measurable and achievable.
- Aligned goals.
- Specific goals created by both leadership and team members on a quarterly basis that support the organizational objective.
- Weekly tracking system.
- Weekly update of everyone's goals based on likelihood of achievement and quality of work.
- Quarterly accountability.
- Marking all goals as "achieved" or "not achieved" at the end of the quarter. Discuss lessons learned and set objectives and goals for the next quarter.

HOW TO USE DATA

Data is just data. It isn't useful unless you harness the information it can provide and then act on it.

You can only do this if you can understand events and outcomes, relationships, and patterns and can translate that into information, knowledge, and wisdom.

A good example is with the weather. You look outside and see it's snowing. That is data. You can't do much about that. But you then determine the temperature just dropped below thirty-two degrees Fahrenheit and the air pressure dropped forty millibars in twenty-four hours. That is information.

But you can't stop there. You note that when the humidity is high and the temperature and pressure are low, it snows. That is knowledge.

Wisdom is when you can predict when it will snow next.

Finally, action is when you decide to dress accordingly and ensure your snow tires are fully inflated so you are best prepared for the weather.

This can be applied to business as well.

Customer Service Data

Data	Information	Knowledge	Wisdom	Action
Customer cancels order.	They canceled their order online because the item wasn't in stock.	When product isn't available, customers cancel their orders.	This occurs 50% of the time.	Stock more inventory to meet demand.

Figure 28-1

Leaders care about knowledge, wisdom, and action. See if you can apply it to the activity that generates data in your business.

KEEPING SCORE

You always need to view your progress and keep score. After all, if you can't measure something and know the results, you can't possibly improve.

Using an everyday analogy, if you are trying to lose weight, don't you need to step on a scale to measure your progress? If not, you really don't know if you are succeeding or not. Similarly, if you are trying to improve your golf game, how do you really know if you are getting better if you aren't keeping score?

So, what are key performance indicators (KPIs) that can be used to measure business progress, and which ones are right for my business?

KPIs are the significant metrics that indicate your progress, but not all of them are the same. First things first about KPIs—you need to make sure they fully align with your business goals.

For example, if a key goal is to increase sales, you need to indicate by how much and when. In other words, your goal is to increase sales by 20 percent in the next calendar year. To accomplish this, you are increasing your marketing budget by 10 percent and are focused on your presence at five industry trade events.

For further clarification, consider the following KPI examples. The first is an online store; the other is a manufacturer.

The online company may care about KPIs such as:

- Conversion rate: Total website visitors purchasing as compared to total website visitors
- Abandonment rate: Rate of users who leave the website without completing their purchase
- Order value: How much each customer spends

The manufacturer may care about a very different set of KPIs, such as:

- Capacity utilization: How much of your available capacity you are using on your production line
- Inventory turnover: How frequently your company sells and replaces its stock of goods during a specific time period
- Customer returns: Number of defective products returned in a certain period

UNIVERSAL KPIS

In the example above, although the specified metrics are different, it does not mean one set is more important than the other. Each has its own important relevance based on the nature of the business doing the measuring. That said, there are some KPIs that are universal to almost every business. The following are the top KPIs to consider.

Revenue

Revenue or sales is the sum of the products or services customers have purchased from your company in a particular period.

Sales data needs to be reviewed against prior periods and go-forward forecasts. Key items that can impact sales and need to be correlated include promotional campaigns, price changes, seasonal forces, and competitors' activities.

Gross Margin

Gross margin is calculated as a company's total sales less direct costs to deliver the sales or cost of goods sold.

Tracking margins is important for growing companies, since increased volumes should improve efficiency and lower the cost per unit.

Monthly Profit/Loss

While increasing sales is a key indicator of a company's health, a company must be profitable to survive, much less prosper.

As a result, it is critical to track the cost of goods sold and fixed/variable costs that impact the bottom line.

Cash Flow

You need to have cash available to pay your bills. Though monthly profit/loss is an indicator of financial health, cash and profits are not the same. Positive cash flow indicates you have more money going into your business at any given time than you do coming out. Profits, on the other hand, indicate revenue and expenses for a period of time, such as the end of a month.

One example of this difference is noting that in January, your business has sales volume of $100,000. Expenses, including rent, payroll, and materials, is $90,000. So, your profit is $10,000. But . . . some clients haven't yet paid their invoices, and some others have paid with a credit card and the payments haven't cleared. So, you actually have $88,000 in cash inflows with $12,000 in receivables, so your net cash flow is –$2,000.

Overhead

Overhead costs are fixed costs that are necessary to run a business but are not correlated with the amount of goods or services produced by the business, such as management salaries or rents being paid per month. Keeping these in line with industry norms is very important. For example, if you have an extra layer of management and your headquarters location is high-end, expensive space, you are likely at a competitive disadvantage.

Customer Retention

Customer loyalty and retention demonstrate that you are attracting the right customers, getting them to buy, and bringing you even more customers.

Being proactive to stay close to the customer is therefore paramount. Common methods for measuring customer loyalty and retention include customer surveys, direct feedback at point of purchase, and purchase analysis.

Customer Acquisition Cost

This metric is a measure of the total cost associated with acquiring a new customer, including all aspects of marketing and sales. Customer acquisition cost is calculated by dividing total acquisition expenses by total new customers over a given period.

Operating Productivity

Having a productive staff is monumentally important. Productivity ratios can be applied to almost any aspect of your business. For example, sales productivity is simply the actual revenue divided by the number of salespeople. You can then compare your productivity to industry norms and monitor continuous improvement by accumulating your statistics over time.

Inventory Turnover

Managing inventory levels is important for companies to show whether sales efforts are effective or whether costs are being controlled. The inventory turnover ratio is an important measure of how well a company generates sales from its inventory.

For growing companies, this is an important area to manage. You will find that you either have too much inventory (cash tied up, high storage costs, obsolescence, and spoilage costs) or not enough (lost sales and lower market share). The challenges include forecasting inventory requirements, buying in cost-effective lot sizes, and just-in-time delivery systems.

For a full list of sixty-eight Financial KPIs & Scorecard Measures, visit www.midcourseadvisors.com/growlikeapro.

<table>
<tr><td>ASSIGNMENT</td><td>Time to pause and put what you learned to work.

Determine the KPIs most appropriate for
your business and track them closely.</td></tr>
</table>

REAL-WORLD EXAMPLES

At USI, we focused on all of these measurements. Most intensely, we cared about cash flow and customer retention and one other measurement not listed above. That was Pitch Success Rate.

Until we disrupted the corporate real estate industry and became a well-known company nationally, we weren't invited to participate in most Requests for Proposal (RFPs) issued by companies, and those that did often didn't want to take a risk with a new, albeit upstart, company.

As a result, we knew we had to win at a higher rate than the established competition, so we put a lot of effort into making the best of these opportunities by closely measuring how/why we succeeded and how/why we didn't.

We also made sure the KPI scorecard was visible. If those who can impact the results can't see the opportunities or challenges, they won't be able to address or impact them nearly as effectively.

PRO POINTERS

- Scalable growth is only achieved with predictable execution—the link between any idea and its implementation.

- For data to be useful, you must understand events and outcomes, relationships, and patterns, and then translate those into information, knowledge, and wisdom.

- In order to achieve any growth, you must be able to measure every part of your business.

- KPIs are the various metrics that can be measured to indicate progress. Different types of businesses and different industries may use an assortment of KPIs. Be sure the ones you choose align with your business goals.

- There are a number of KPIs that are universal to every business, including:

  o Revenue
  o Gross Margin
  o Monthly Profit/Loss
  o Cash Flow
  o Overhead
  o Customer Retention
  o Customer Acquisition Cost
  o Operating Productivity
  o Inventory Turnover

Chapter 29

MAKE IT VISIBLE

"If a tree falls in the forest and no one is
around to hear it, does it make a sound?"

—Unknown

If no one knows or sees the KPIs, then why implement them and measure?

It is really important that every key stakeholder who can contribute to the success of the company has visibility to metrics.

Sure, not everyone needs to see every metric, but there are certain ones everyone must see. They include those that:

- Demonstrate progress of the company as a whole, so the employees can see how the company's overall goals and vision are aligned with ongoing plans and strategies
- Demonstrate progress of the individual or team for which they are providing work effort to impact their department and company as a whole

The most capable department heads demonstrate the connection between the individual/department and the whole. That way team members can see how their contributions matter and how their compensation can be impacted (positively and negatively).

As suggested in Chapter 25, having a balanced scorecard is a good way to demonstrate all the key areas you are measuring and want to make visible.

The key categories include Financial, Customer, Learning, and Growth and Internal. An example dashboard is shown in Figure 29-1.

Balanced Scorecard

BALANCED SCORECARD AS OF APRIL 30, 2019

FINANCIAL	Target	Current	% of Target
Increase Total Revenue	$5.00	$2.00	40%
Increase Net Profit	$1.00	$0.50	50%
Increase Profit Margin	$0.20	$0.25	125%
Increase Profit per Customer	1.3%	0.9%	70%

CUSTOMER	Target	Current	% of Target
Increase Total Customer	80	57	71%
Increase Customer Retention	75	55	73%
Increase Customer Satisfaction	95	85	89%
Increase Referrals	10	2	20%

LEARNING & GROWTH	Target	Current	% of Target
Open New Sales Regions	3	1	33%
Develop New Service Line	2	1	50%
Train Mgmt. on Tetramap	15	5	33%
Centralize Training Team	1	0	0%

INTERNAL	Target	Current	% of Target
Reduce Employee Turnover	25	10	40%
Fill Vacancies	45	25	56%
Add Diversity to Team	20	10	50%
Reduce Avg. Overtime	30	30	100%

Figure 29-1

If you lead a department that delivers a product that is responsible for a $1 million increase in annual revenue, that is 20 percent of the $5 million total. If your team is below the 40 percent current target progress, you know you are pulling the rest of the team down and need to further step up your game. On the other hand, if you are ahead of schedule, maybe you can do more to help others who aren't doing as well.

Visibility and transparency help. Make it happen.

PRO POINTERS

- If no one knows the score, then implementing and measuring KPIs is a waste of everyone's time.

- The metrics that must be shared with everyone include those that demonstrate overall company progress as well as those that demonstrate the progress of the individual or team.

- A balanced scorecard approach is a good way to share and make visible all key areas.

- Visibility and transparency are part of every successful organization.

Decision

Value catalysts

Sale

Resources

Business Durability

Positioning

DEVELOP AN EXIT PLAN

Chapter 30

KNOW YOUR END GAME FIRST

"If you don't know where you're going,
you may wind up someplace else."

— Yogi Berra
Hall of Fame New York Yankee
Catcher and Prophet

As a young man, in the 1920s, my grandfather worked as a vendor at Yankee Stadium. Yes, he saw Babe Ruth and Lou Gehrig play. So, I had no choice but to be a Yankee fan. As a result, I had to pick a Yankee quote to include somewhere in this book, and I think the one I've chosen here is pretty applicable.

In my career, I have worked with and for dozens and dozens of executives. I always ask these executives if they have a personal financial advisor and plan. Almost all say they do intend to plan for their retirement. Doing so enables them to take a longer-term view to balance their appetite for risk and reward.

So, the answers I receive always surprise me when I speak to these same executives about having a plan, one that is beyond an annual budget, for their businesses. Most suggest they don't have any sort of exit plan because they have to be focused on the near term and the business environment keeps changing so quickly.

Believe me, I get it.

It is understandable, since they need to please their stakeholders, including owners, managers, employees, and customers, and it needs to be done now. If you work for and eventually lead a company, understand that companies have multiple stakeholders, including employees, customers, business partners, and the communities within which they operate.

Nevertheless, let me suggest that not planning for the exit is a mission-critical error. In fact, it can derail your focus and therefore your success.

If you may want to sell your business at some point, you need to know when you may wish to do so. Based on the timing or decision, you need to think about what buyers or investors value once you leave. They value elements that generate predictable success, including the quality and depth of a leadership team that can run the business; resources like cash, technology, and real estate; processes and tools used to consistently manage the business; and a value proposition, profitability, and market share that enable business durability.

Far too many executives and owners approach me suggesting they want to sell now or within the next year or two, sometimes prompted by an unexpected health issue for them or a loved one. Maybe the business isn't doing so well and they realize they want to retire. Maybe they just want the cash. Whatever the reason, it takes time and planning well before the time you want to sell to have an exit strategy. Unfortunately, most leaders are unfortunately unprepared.

The first thing to consider is your end game. That determines your path. You want to be able to:

- Leave the company on the date you choose
- Leave the company to the successor you choose

- Leave the company with the amount of cash you desire to secure a comfortable post-business life

Figure 30-1 demonstrates the thinking behind planning needs to go from end to beginning, or Exit to Goals.

Exit Planning Ladder

Exit	Succession	Growth	Strategy	Goals
☐ Decision	☐ Develop Team	☐ Focus	☐ Market Penetration	☐ Sales
☐ Team		☐ Scale		☐ Revenue
☐ Resources	☐ Identify Next Leaders	☐ Leverage	☐ Market Expansion	☐ Profit
☐ Processes		☐ Partners	☐ Product Expansion	☐ Cash Flow
☐ Business Durability	☐ Build Legacy	☐ Metrics		☐ Market Share
	☐ Timeline	☐ Automation	☐ Diversify	
☐ Sale		☐ References	☐ Acquisition	☐ Operation Efficiency
		☐ Reinvest		

Figure 30-1

To assess exit-planning needs, you should address the following questions:

- Have you determined a date, financial parameters, and a successor to exit the company?
- Do you have a stable and motivated management team fully capable of running the company in your absence?
- Does your company have plans to protect it from the performance or departure of one or more key employees?
- Do you have proper incentives for team members aligned with increasing the value of your company?

- Do your current compensation programs promote the retention of key team members?
- Do you have the right processes and systems to effectively manage the business in a consistent and high-quality manner and support further growth?
- Do you have an established and varied customer base?
- Do you have recurring and diverse revenue streams to protect the company from a downturn?
- Do you have strong financial controls?
- Do you have a realistic, documented growth strategy that aligns with your overall business and exit plan?

Note this isn't limited to private company executives and owners. To leave the greatest legacy, ensuring your good work endures and having the strongest exit package, you need to have all of these elements in place as well. So, plan ahead for the exit.

Once you have recognized the needs associated with exit planning, you can address succession, growth, strategy, and goals. As you've reached the end of the book, you know that the elements of these critical steps are detailed in other chapters. Now, knowing that you should start with the end in mind, go back and review as needed.

As Zig Ziglar has suggested, "You will get all you want in life if you help people enough people and get what they want." I would suggest you also need to know what to do when you wish to exit the company and move on to another venture, retire, or seek some other opportunities.

ASSIGNMENT

Time to pause and put what you learned to work.

Answer the questions above and create an outline for your exit plan.

PRO POINTERS

- Not planning for your end game early in your journey is a mission-critical error.

- An exit strategy takes time and planning throughout the journey in order to be successful.

- Determine your path—leave at the time you choose with the right team, resources, processes, and durability in place.

- With proactive and ongoing planning, you will have all of the components in place to depart on your terms.

Chapter 31

PUTTING IT ALL TOGETHER

"Don't mistake activity with achievement."

—*John Wooden*
Hall of Fame College Basketball Coach

As suggested in the beginning of the book, building a thriving business and sustaining it is neither easy nor for the faint of heart.

I've discussed numerous proven methodologies and tools that can be used to help your business progress. As you read the book, you may have thought that these methodologies and tools are intended to make sure leaders do the right things to increase their odds to successfully grow their businesses.

Though that argument can certainly be made, the real reason is to avoid costly mistakes that can drain or put you out of business.

If you make an error identifying a problem or you create a solution that doesn't address a problem, this will be a costly mistake.

If you fail to target the right customer and try to sell to those who won't likely buy and consume your products and services, this will be a costly mistake.

If you have a great product and/or service that solves a needed problem, but no one knows about it and therefore can't buy it, this will be a costly mistake.

If you know how to sell but don't know how to manage the end-to-end process, this will be a costly mistake.

If you don't hire the right people and help them to develop and advance, especially in today's low unemployment market, this will be a costly mistake.

If you connect with a number of partners, but they divert your efforts and don't actually extend your reach, this will be a costly mistake.

If you don't know how to secure, invest, and manage your finances, this will be a costly mistake.

If you recreate the wheel with every operational requirement, this will be a costly mistake.

If you fail to measure and learn from what you are doing, this will be a costly mistake.

And finally, if you don't know where you are ultimately heading by developing an exit plan now, this will be a costly mistake.

Feel free to find additional resources at www.midcourseadvisors.com/growlikeapro.

You can also reach me directly at agoldstrom@midcourseadvisors.com or 770-633-2260.

I welcome all inquiries.

ACKNOWLEDGMENTS

Success in business and in life does not come without the support of numerous people.

But it is very easy to identify the one person who has helped me the most. That person is my wife, Lori.

Simply, I could not have pursued my entrepreneurial journey without her unwavering support. When we both recognized I had a lot of ideas and energy, she gladly agreed that I would be the primary breadwinner and she would be the primary caregiver in our family.

She didn't have to do that; she had a law degree and was successful in the world of trusts and estates. But her maternal instinct was greater than her career motivations. We now have two great, grown-up young women as a result.

But, once the choice was made, we were both all in.

When she was pregnant with our first child and due in only one week, she consented to me traveling out of the area to an important business meeting as long as I could hop on a plane if she went into labor.

When I needed to spend a good portion of our end-of-year holidays in a Kinkos (now FedEx Office) to complete a proposal for a significant piece of business, she said, "Do what you need to do."

When I needed to spend most of 2012 out of the country to address a significant global business challenge, she said, "Take some time to visit some other locations while you are away."

Certainly, my relationship with my wife and kids goes far beyond simply her accommodating my business needs without hesitation. We've been happily married for more than twenty-seven years, and we have enjoyed many great moments and also endured a number of challenges together.

For purposes of this dedication and this book, Lori was by far and away the most important person in my professional journey.

I love you, Lori.

ABOUT THE AUTHOR

As managing partner at Midcourse Advisors, Andy Goldstrom and his team grow companies profitably and do it fast. Andy is an expert at selling and serving in the real estate and other industries and is a sought-after business partner and speaker.

Early in his career, Andy started and built a division of a real estate brokerage company that generated 30 percent–plus margins. After that, he took over an existing real estate business and grew the top line from $70 million to $100 million and profit from $10 million to $17 million in three years. Both businesses were both designated as Inc. 500 companies, the fastest-growing privately held companies nationwide, and subsequently sold to Fortune 500 companies at high multiples. Most recently, he served as global director at a major investment bank, where he grew service capabilities in seventy countries while saving $12 million annually.

In each case, Andy led sales teams that competed efficiently and effectively to win an extraordinary amount of business. In addition, he reduced cycle times and increased the frequency of incoming sustainable business, creating incremental value that was monetized when the companies were sold.

He started Midcourse Advisors to help leaders bolster their companies and now offers his knowledge and experience to organizations looking for ways to grow and improve.

Andy also serves as an instructor in entrepreneurship at Georgia State University in Atlanta, Georgia. He has been inspired by students who offer unique perspectives in today's digital economy.

Andy is an aspiring comedian. He did this to honor his late father, who enjoyed comedy, and also challenge himself. A couple of his very amateur performances can be found on YouTube.

Finally, Andy lives in Marietta, Georgia, with his wife, Lori, and his two dogs, Calhoun and Summer. He has two grown children, Sarah and Audrey.

MORE INFORMATION ON MIDCOURSE ADVISORS' SERVICES

1-TO-1 COACHING

Midcourse Advisors has the people, process, and platforms to deliver highly impactful individualized and tailored services to help you and your company grow faster and more profitably.

We offer a hands-on culture and deep experience that has propelled multiple companies to Inc. 500 growth levels.

By meeting face to face and/or via video conference for a period of months, we can help you make appropriate adjustments to your business that you can implement and see immediate results.

To learn more about how we work with our coaching clients, please visit www.midcourseadvisors.com/coach.

GROUP COACHING

For those who wish to benefit from Midcourse Advisors' programs and would wish to do so more economically in a group setting, our Group Coaching program is for you.

These meetings are held via video conference and offer direct feedback from Midcourse Advisors coaches together with others in your limited group.

To learn more about how we work with our group coaching clients, please visit www.midcourseadvisors.com/groupcoach.

ONLINE PROGRAM

If you want to learn on your own and apply our tools and methodologies on your own, you can access our training modules online.

To learn more about our online program, please visit www.midcourseadvisors.com/onlinecourses.

SPEAKING

When you want to inspire a group to help grow your company fast and profitably, you need a presenter who can provide entertaining, practical, and readily implementable strategies.

Whether at your local office, regional meeting, or national conference, our presentations win both hearts and minds of attendees that will have an immediate and lasting impact on your business.

To learn more about our presentation options, please visit www.midcoursadvisors.com/speaking.

PODCASTS

There are a number of great podcasts out there in the business and growth spaces.

To learn more about having Andy Goldstrom or someone from his team on your podcast, please visit www.midcourseadvisors.com/podcasts.